£3·75

D1356085

MEGALITHIC LUNAR
OBSERVATORIES

MEGALITHIC LUNAR OBSERVATORIES

BY

A. THOM

OXFORD
AT THE CLARENDON PRESS

Oxford University Press, Walton Street, Oxford OX2 6DP

OXFORD LONDON GLASGOW
NEW YORK TORONTO MELBOURNE WELLINGTON
KUALA LUMPUR SINGAPORE JAKARTA HONG KONG TOKYO
DELHI BOMBAY CALCUTTA MADRAS KARACHI
IBADAN NAIROBI DAR ES SALAAM CAPE TOWN

ISBN 0 19 858132 7

© *Oxford University Press 1971*

First published 1971
Reprinted 1973 (with corrections), 1978

All rights reserved. No part of this publication may be repro-
duced, stored in a retrieval system, or transmitted, in any form
or by any means, electronic, mechanical, photocopying, recording,
or otherwise, without the prior permission of
Oxford University Press

Printed in Great Britain
at the University Press, Oxford
by Vivian Ridler
Printer to the University

PREFACE

In a previous volume (*Megalithic sites in Britain*, 1967) I have given details of an investigation into the metrology, geometry, and astronomy of the builders of the Megalithic sites in Britain. There I gave also a résumé of the background of statistics, mathematics, and astronomy necessary to an understanding of the sites. Although I have assumed that the reader of the present volume has some knowledge of descriptive astronomy a brief description is given of those parts of the subject that bear on the movements of the Moon in the sky. This has been augmented throughout the text by simple explanations.

The reader who does not want to go into the subject in great detail can, I suggest, omit certain sections: the analysis at the end of Chapter 4 (solstitial sites), all of Chapter 3 (refraction), and the latter part of Chapter 7 dealing with parallax. Chapter 6 is a record of sites that are perhaps individually of less importance and need not be read in detail by the general reader.

As the investigation advanced it became evident that I was not dealing with monuments orientated for some ritualistic purpose but rather with the remnants of a scientific study of the Moon's motion. When this is recognized it will be found that a great mass of material falls into place. We must no longer assert that these people could not possibly have known this or done that. It has proved much more fruitful to ask ourselves how a trained scientific mind would have approached their problems, always bearing in mind the kind of facilities which were available.

It is perhaps too much to hope that every numerical value given here is accurate, but several of the important sites on which the main arguments are based have been visited time after time until the azimuths, etc. could be fully checked by repeated independent astronomical determinations.

A slight change has been made in the nomenclature used in *Megalithic sites*. What I have previously called the lunar solstice is here called the lunar standstill. This is such an important concept that it is a pity that a better name does not exist.

When comparisons are made with the declinations listed in *Megalithic sites* it should be noted that there, for uniformity, all declinations were computed without the application of parallax. As the present volume deals mainly with the Moon and the Sun, lunar or solar parallax has been applied. Where real differences are found between measurements now given and those previously published it indicates that a new and more accurate survey has given slightly different results.

The research on which this book is based was made possible by a grant from the C. T. Lloyd Foundation, Cleveland, Ohio, and by assistance from the Butkin Foundation, Cleveland, Ohio. I am deeply indebted to both these foundations and to Mr. Robert L. Merritt for help in a variety of ways.

My thanks are also due to a number of people who helped with the surveys. I gratefully acknowledge the assistance of the map-room staff of the Bodleian Library, Oxford, the library of the Society of Antiquaries of Scotland, the Archaeological Department of the Ordnance Survey, Edinburgh, and H.M. Nautical Almanac Office, Herstmonceux Castle.

During the preparation of the manuscript I had much fruitful discussion with Dr. A. E. Roy, Dr. A. S. Thom, Brigadier A. Prain, and Miss M. Campbell. I must also mention those members of the staff of the Clarendon Press who helped so much with the final layout of both of my books.

A.T.

Dunlop, Ayrshire
November 1969

CONTENTS

LIST OF MAIN SYMBOLS

(Page references are to definitions)

δ   declination (p. 117)

φ   latitude (p. 22)

H   hour angle (p. 117) (but in Chapter 3 H is used for height difference in feet)

Az.   azimuth (p. 21)

h   altitude (p. 21)

ε   obliquity of ecliptic (p. 15)

i   inclination of Moon's orbit to ecliptic (Fig. 2.1)

T   terrestrial refraction (p. 28)

T″   terrestrial refraction in seconds of arc (p. 30)

R   astronomical refraction (p. 28)

L   distance to foresight in feet (p. 30)

D   distance to foresight in miles (p. 31)

s   semidiameter

Δ   perturbation, usually about 9 arc minutes (p. 18)

p   (in Chapter 7) parallax

2p   (in Chapter 8) stake movement in the day at the declination maximum

K   (in Chapter 3) refraction coefficient (but it is used differently in Chapter 8)

1

INTRODUCTION

1.1. WE do not know the extent of Megalithic man's knowledge of geometry and astronomy. Perhaps we never shall. He was a competent engineer. Witness how he could set out large projects to an accuracy approaching 1 in 1000, and how he could transport and erect blocks of stone weighing up to 50 tons. He had an extensive knowledge of practical geometry, and used the 3, 4, 5 right-angle triangle extensively. He also knew the 5, 12, 13 right-angle triangle, the 8, 15, 17, and the 12, 35, 37. There is a suspicion that he also knew the 9, 40, 41. He had in addition discovered many other triangles with integral sides that satisfied very closely the Pythagorean relation. These triangles were used in a peculiar geometry, in which he constructed rings, set out in stone, of various shapes: circular, egg-shaped, elliptical, etc. These constructions were made according to two rules: all linear dimensions had to be integral multiples of the unit, and the perimeters had to be multiples of $2\frac{1}{2}$ units. The unit was the Megalithic yard (MY) of length $2\cdot720\pm0\cdot003$ feet.

But Megalithic man could also work on a much smaller scale. Amongst the 'cup and ring' marks found incised on stones and rocks throughout Britain, we find a similar geometry with the same rules, but applied with even greater ingenuity. From a statistical examination of scores of these in Scotland there emerges another unit with a length of $0\cdot816$ inches, which is exactly one-fortieth of the Megalithic yard. To set out these small designs on polished rock demanded the use of trammels or beam compasses with the points set correctly to within a few thousandths of an inch. The obsession with lengths that were multiples of the unit probably arose because adjustable trammels were not available. Sets of trammels were probably constructed with the points set at, say, 2, $2\frac{1}{2}$, 3, $3\frac{1}{2}$, etc. units apart.

It is obvious that behind all this must have lain a solid background of technological knowledge. Here I am not thinking only of his knowledge of ceramics, textiles, tanning, carpentry, husbandry, metallurgy, and the like, but of his knowledge of levers, fulcrums, foundations, sheerlegs, slings, and ropes. Involved in his linear metrology was his knowledge of how to make accurate measuring rods, shape the ends, and use them accurately. There is evidence that he did not use the slope length on the ground, but the horizontal distance, as does a modern surveyor, and that he could 'range in' a straight line between mutually invisible points. There was also his ability to build and use boats: he travelled freely as far as Shetland, crossing the wide stretch of open water north of Orkney, as well as the exceedingly dangerous Pentland Firth and the North Channel between Kintyre and Ireland. This involved a knowledge of the tides and tidal currents that rule these waters.

1.2. The author has for nearly fifty summers sailed on the west coast of Britain and can claim to know it intimately from the Mull of Kintyre to the Butt of Lewis. The navigation of these waters by small craft is conditioned completely by the tidal currents and tide rips that abound. The flood tide sweeping up the west coast of Europe is split by Ireland. When it comes together again it is some six hours out of phase and so produces an amphidromic point opposite the Mull of Kintyre. This means that high water on one side of Kintyre takes place when it is low water on the other. The result is that the water oscillates to and fro round the Mull. As at any amphidromic point, the tidal range is small but the speed of the streams is violent. When the seas running in from the Western Ocean meet the west-going stream they are shortened and heightened until they break. Tide rips of this kind can be produced at any exposed headland or any formation that allows a fast-moving stream to meet the sea. In bad weather no open boat can survive in these tide rips. The danger is that a boat capable of being moved by oar or paddle at only a slow speed may be drawn into such a tide race and destroyed.

Thus it behoves the would-be navigator to make his passage at such time as the tide permits. He must know in advance how the stream will be running and how long it will last. During spring tides the speed of the streams and the violence of the sea are very much greater than at neaps. It may be necessary to choose the time for a crossing to be at neaps, or, if the journey is to be made with the tide, it may be possible to travel faster and further with a spring tide. The relation between the phase of the Moon and the time, direction, and violence of the tide must be clearly understood.

Enough has been said to show that anyone using these waters regularly would want to know about the tides and so about the Moon. In Chapter 4 we shall discuss four complementary solstitial sites, one being in Jura and the others on the mainland. In Chapter 6 a group of lunar sites will be described scattered over Jura, Gigha, and Kintyre (see Fig. 11.1, p. 115). Evidently there was much coming and going across the Sound of Jura. This sound is narrowest at its northern end, but it is just here that the danger of being sucked into the Gulf of Corriebhreckan, between Jura and Scarba, by the *west*-running flood tide is at its greatest. The Gulf is almost as well known as the Maelstrom. Any small craft, even if decked, that is swept through by the flood (and there is no turning back) against the seas raised by a westerly gale, has little chance of survival in the terrific seas that break from the whirlpool for several miles to the west. The author has on several occasions coming through at slack water seen the start of the whirlpool, and knows what a frightening sight it can be.

1.3. At an early stage men living on the coasts of the Western Ocean must have noticed the connection between the tides and the Moon. Probably this connection was one of the factors that caused Megalithic man to study the movements of the Moon. It is the principal object of this book to show that he carried this study much further, until he was able to predict which full or new Moon would give rise to an eclipse of the Moon or of the Sun.

But to make accurate predictions one must have an accurate calendar. It has been shown elsewhere (Thom 1967) that Megalithic man made use of a calendar linked to the Sun. In some Mediterranean countries the calendar was based on the heliacal risings of certain bright stars. Such a calendar does not have anything like the accuracy of Megalithic man's calendar, which could not get out of step with the Sun by more than a day, if as much. The further north one is, the easier it is to mark a given day in the year by establishing a foresight for the setting Sun on that day. This is because the range of the setting point throughout the year increases with latitude, until in Scotland it is twice as great as in tropical countries. Ideally the calendar is based on observations of the Sun made at the equinoxes, when the daily movement of the setting Sun along the horizon is a maximum and of the order of its own diameter, but we find other dates marked, dividing the year into sixteen parts. A comparison of the observed declinations with those of the ideal sixteen-month calendar shows (Thom 1967, chapter 9) that we have here Megalithic man's calendar.

1.4. We find two kinds of solar or lunar sight lines. There are those of the true observatories, where, as we shall see, by making skilful use of distant natural foresights it was possible to detect changes of declination of a few seconds of arc. Then there are those sites where an arrangement of stones indicates the rising or setting point without any distant and therefore accurate foresight. Stonehenge, Woodhenge, and Castle Rigg probably all belong to the second class. This kind of indication needs to consist of widely separated stones to give any accuracy. It is true that artificial sights (cf. hole stones) on the stones would have increased the accuracy, or perishable foresights of wood or earth on the horizon may have existed at some sites. But anyone looking along the various sight lines at Castle Rigg will see that the horizon is generally distant and is unlikely to have lent itself to such an arrangement. Various bits of evidence suggest, however, that certain sites contained vertical wooden poles. Perhaps all did; large stakes must have been used during the construction. Two stakes 3 inches in diameter and 1000 feet apart define an azimuth to about an arc minute and so declination to about one-half of this—assuming a clean-cut horizon free from scrub and trees. But timber perishes, and if this kind of sighting device had been intended to last one would expect to find stone sockets, so that the poles could be accurately replaced. So far such sockets have been seen at one or two places only.

In connection with our present study, Castle Rigg is worth looking at. Details will be found elsewhere (Thom 1967). Here we may say that it is basically a standard Type A flattened circle but has all the construction points and all the 30° points marked by stones on the circumference. This brings stones diametrically opposite, an arrangement that was usually avoided. It was perhaps liable to cause confusion unless, as at Castle Rigg, the diameter was intended to indicate a rising or setting point of a celestial body. Castle Rigg shows five solar lines and three lunar. It is noteworthy that the builders succeeded in so placing the circle that no less than five of these are formed by lines belonging to the geometrical construction. This was achieved by making use of the varying altitude of the mountain horizon. The time and effort that must have been expended by the builders on this remarkable achievement show a desire to combine in a peculiar way their geometry and astronomy. When we compare Castle Rigg with, say, Temple Wood, we see the great difference between the two kinds of site and the two kinds of sight line. Temple Wood—functional, scientific; Castle Rigg—symbolic, mystical.

Castle Rigg, however, shows another feature found elsewhere. Diametrically opposite to the outlier there is a stone in the perimeter, at a point where one would not expect a stone to be, drawing attention to the fact that the outlier is to be viewed from this stone over the centre. Sometimes circles occur in groups, and this conventional arrangement would have prevented an outlier being viewed from the wrong circle. The Castle Rigg outlier is far enough away to make the calendar day to which it belongs quite definite, but the other lines across the circle do not provide this kind of accuracy, and are useless for our present study.

The known sites capable of the kind of accuracy required are mostly in Scotland. There are relatively few places in England from which one can see a clean-cut horizon of the kind that might provide suitable foresights. For example, Stanton Drew has most of its horizon tree-covered. An examination of the tables shows how the lunar sites spread from Galloway over Argyllshire and its islands to an important set in the Outer Hebrides. We also find some on the east coast and a very important set in Caithness. There is one in Pembrokeshire, and it seems likely that the stones that were formerly in several groups on the Glastonbury heights made use of the Black Mountain in Wales as an accurate foresight. It does not seem possible yet to specify exactly the position of the backsight, so this site has not been used.

It is interesting to note how many of the lunar backsights are marked by very tall stones. It is probably true to say that nearly all the impressive alignments in Britain are lunar, an important exception being the Nine Maidens alignment in Cornwall. It is evident that great importance was attached to the lunar sites. When we understand that years of work went into fixing the exact spot where a backsight should be placed, we begin to appreciate why it was important to mark the spot well and permanently. Perhaps there were vandals in those days also, but Megalithic vandals would hesitate about tackling stones of the size used at many of the sites. The officially approved and organized vandalism of recent centuries has been much more effective.

1.5. Many of the lunar sites are in inaccessible situations, and could only be reached carrying the specially lightened theodolite normally used for my older surveys. It has, however, become apparent that the solstitial and lunar sites demanded better equipment. Accordingly, when possible, a heavier theodolite reading to 20″ is now used. It cannot be carried so far, but nevertheless some sites have been remeasured along with those recently found or recently recognized as lunar. In general the azimuth determinations are of sufficient accuracy, but some of the hill horizons may still be found wanting. The foresight of every lunar site ought eventually to be measured to ±1′ in azimuth and ±20″ in altitude.

1.6. Method by which the observations were made

A great many of the descriptions to be given later of sites and the theory underlying their use will be obscure unless the method used by Megalithic man to take his observations is clearly understood. He had no instruments with accurately graduated circles, but made use of the great circle of the horizon. Instead of graduations he used foresights on the horizon, which were usually natural, and far enough away to permit of great accuracy. As the foresight could not in general be moved about, he moved the backsight. A cleft or notch in a distant horizon can give a precision, as we shall see, as great as that attained in the graduations of a good theodolite, and far in excess of, say, a prismatic compass.

We shall illustrate the method by considering the Moon setting in the northwest near the most northerly position it can reach at that particular lunation. The same method applies to the Sun or Moon rising or setting.

The observer stands in such a position that the Moon will, as it goes down, graze a distant foresight, in Fig. 1.1 assumed to be a hilltop. As the orb slides past the hill he makes the final adjustments to his position to get exact contact between one or other limb and an unambiguous point on the hill profile. He marks the final position by a stake or rod. This procedure he repeats for several nights about the time of maximum declination, i.e. about the time when the Moon attains its most northerly setting position. In practice it may be that all the stakes are set out on the line AA, which lies across the line of sight, but need not be exactly at right angles to it. But to avoid confusion we shall assume that he steps back a short constant distance each night. Setting the stake on Monday at M, the position on Tuesday is not on AA but at T. He thus sets out a curve on the ground. The point furthest to the

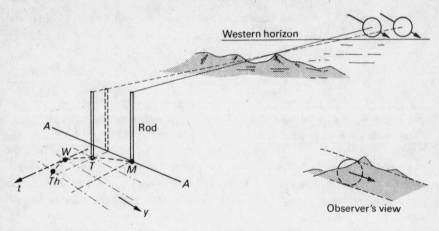

FIG. 1.1. The method of observing.

left corresponds to the furthest north position attained by the Moon at that particular lunation.

If the observer did step back each night, the curve obtained on the ground is, to some scale, a graph of the Moon's declination plotted on a time base. We know that at least for the Sun he did not always step back (cf. Kintraw, § 4.2). He may never have; but it will make descriptions easier to follow if we assume that we are dealing with a curve rather than allowing all the stake positions to pile on to one line. Remember that the stake position moves first in one direction and then in the other.

When later in the book the term 'stake position' is used, it is to be understood that it refers to a stake position obtained by the above method.

2

ASTRONOMICAL BACKGROUND

2.1. IN this chapter we shall give a description of the astronomical concepts needed for an understanding of Megalithic man's observatories. For those unfamiliar with astronomical terms some descriptive, if not rigid, definitions are given in Appendix A.

In the past, two distinct astronomical methods of dating Megalithic sites have been attempted. Both presuppose that when the site was built there was a known foresight behind which a known star (or the Sun) rose or set. The star method depends on the fact that the precession of the equinoxes causes a star's declination to alter slowly with the passing of the centuries. If the declination of the foresight is measured, we obtain the date of the erection of the site. This method is discussed in Thom 1967, and need not be considered further here. The second method assumes that there is an accurate foresight for the Sun at the solstice. Since the declination of the Sun is then equal to the obliquity of the ecliptic (ϵ), and since this changes very slowly, it seems at first sight that this method is incapable of any accuracy.

For many years astronomers have accepted Newcomb's study of observations of the Sun as giving the most reliable estimate of how the obliquity is changing and has changed in the past. Here we shall use a more recent determination of ϵ by de Sitter (1938), which in fact gives values that differ from Newcomb's, even as far back as 2000 B.C., by only a few seconds of arc. De Sitter's formula is

$$\epsilon = 23° 27' 8''\cdot29 - 47''\cdot080\,t - 0''\cdot0059\,t^2 + 0''\cdot00186\,t^3, \qquad (2.1)$$

where t is measured in centuries *forward* from A.D. 1900. Some values calculated by this formula are given in Table 2.1.

Table 2.1. *Variation of obliquity* ϵ

	t	ϵ	Change in 100 years
1900 B.C.	−38	23° 55′ 6″·72	
1800 B.C.	−37	23° 54′ 27″·96	38″·76
1700 B.C.	−36	23° 53′ 48″·74	39″·22
1600 B.C.	−35	23° 53′ 9″·11	39″·63

Thus during the centuries in which we are here interested ϵ was decreasing by about 40 seconds per century. It follows that if we hope to determine the mean date of the erection of the sites to within a century, we must find from the sight lines values of ϵ with a precision greater than an arc minute. One of the objects of this book is to show that there is a real possibility of approaching this kind of accuracy (a) from Megalithic man's solar observatories and (b) indirectly from his lunar observatories.

The Moon's orbit round the Earth is inclined to the ecliptic at an angle i. Astronomers tell us that the *mean* value of i is $5° 8' 43''$ and that, by dynamical calculation, they have reason to believe that this value has remained constant for hundreds, perhaps thousands, of years. A second object of this book is to show how we can determine an accurate value of i by an analysis of numbers of Megalithic remains in this country and that the value so obtained is within a few seconds of the above value. But the records in stone left us by these people do more. They show us that the erectors were well aware of the phenomena that result from the fact that, while the mean value of i is constant, its actual value oscillates regularly with a small amplitude Δ of amount about 9 arc minutes and a period of half an eclipse year, i.e. $346·6/2$ or $173·3$ days.

2.2. When we look at the sky we see the heavenly bodies as if they were painted on the inside of a hollow sphere viewed from the centre. The nearest approach to depicting such a sphere is a planetarium. But in a book such a device is not possible and it is conventional to imagine ourselves outside and draw the sphere as it then appears. This method of presentation is used in Fig. 2.1, where we see the Earth rotating at the centre of the sphere—the celestial sphere. The plane of the equator extended to the sphere cuts it in the great circle shown. Similarly the plane in which the Sun appears to move round us (the ecliptic) becomes a great circle, i.e. a circle bisecting the sphere. We see the Moon's orbit as a great circle intersecting the plane of the ecliptic in the line of nodes $N_1 N_2$ at an angle i. Looking at the sky our senses do not convey to us the fact that the Sun is very much further away than the Moon and very much larger. Both happen to subtend about the same angle and so both are shown on the celestial sphere as discs of equal size.

In Fig. 2.1 we see how, as viewed from the Earth, the Sun travelling once a year round the ecliptic rises 'up' through the equator at Υ, the First Point of Aries, at the vernal equinox, to attain its maximum declination (ϵ) at the summer solstice. The line of nodes $N_1 N_2$ of the Moon's orbit rotates slowly in the ecliptic, in the direction shown, once in $18·61$ years. When N_1 is at Υ the angles i and ϵ are additive, so that the Moon's orbit is inclined at $(\epsilon+i)$ to the equator, and the Moon's maximum declination then has this value. Half a circuit later, i.e. after $9·3$ years, N_2 is at Υ and the inclination is $(\epsilon-i)$.

If the Moon's orbit were not inclined to the ecliptic there would be an eclipse of the Sun at every new Moon, and every full Moon would be eclipsed. As things are, the two discs can come together only when the Sun is near one of the nodes. But relative to a node the Sun revolves in 346·6 days, called an eclipse year, and so the interval between what we shall call the danger times,

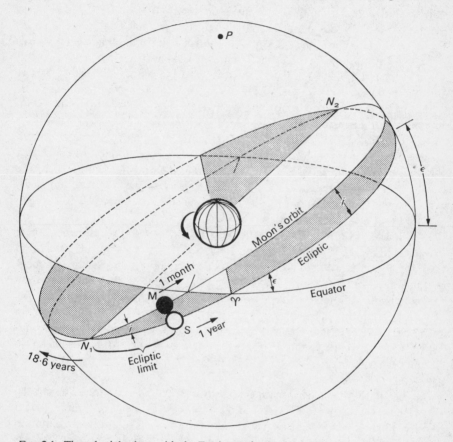

FIG. 2.1. The celestial sphere with the Earth rotating at the centre. S = Sun, M = Moon.

when eclipses can happen, is 173·3 days. In Fig. 2.1 we see the Moon overtaking the Sun (new Moon), but just failing to eclipse it. The Sun has in fact just reached the safe distance from the node, called the ecliptic limit. When the Sun is inside the limit there may be an eclipse, partial or total, but it will be remembered that an eclipse of the Sun can be total only when the observer happens to be in a narrow zone on the Earth's surface, and this zone is different for every eclipse. There is a similar ecliptic limit for eclipses of the Moon, the Sun and Moon then being 180° apart.

From N_1 to N_2 the Sun is 'below' the orbit of the Moon and so it is exerting a 'downward' pull on both the Moon and the Earth. During this half-year, provided the revolving Moon is in the part of its orbit nearer to the Sun, it experiences a greater downward pull than the Earth. But when it is on the far side of its orbit relative to the Sun conditions are reversed. It can be shown dynamically that the ultimate result is that the actual orbit goes through a complete cycle, 9' down and 9' up, while the Sun is going from node to node, i.e. in half an eclipse year. In modern Europe, including classical Europe, the first astronomer to detect this cyclical perturbation or wobble was Tycho Brahé (b. 1546), who pointed out that its maximum occurs when the Sun is at N_1 and again when it is at N_2, i.e. in the middle of the eclipse danger times, exactly as it should do according to modern theory. We may here quote Godfray (2nd edn. 1859, p. 116):

'Tycho Brahé further discovered that the inclination of the lunar orbit to the ecliptic was not a constant quantity of 5° as Hipparchus had supposed, but that it had a mean value of 5° 8', and ranged through 9' 30" on each side of this, the least inclination 4° 58½' occurring when the node was in quadrature, and the greatest 5° 17½' being attained when the node was in syzygy.'

In a footnote Godfray adds:

'Ebn Jounis, an Arabian astronomer (died A.D. 1008), whose works were translated about 30 years since by Mons. Sedillot, states that the inclination of the moon's orbit had been often observed by Aboul-Hassan-Aly-ben-Amajour about the year 918, and that the results he had obtained were generally greater than the 5° of Hipparchus, but that they *varied considerably*.'

It thus appears that the movement, a study of which formed the main reason for Megalithic observatories, was unknown in modern Europe until the sixteenth century, but had been suspected by the Arabs in the tenth century.

2.3. Let us now see what happens to the Moon's declination. During the course of a year the Sun's declination oscillates between the limits $+\epsilon$ and $-\epsilon$. If the lunar orbit were not inclined to the ecliptic, the Moon's declination would go through the same cycle, but in a month instead of a year. But, as we have shown above, the limits vary between $\pm(\epsilon+i)$ and $\pm(\epsilon-i)$. This is shown in Fig. 2.2. We propose in this book to call the time when the limits are $\pm(\epsilon+i)$ the *major standstill* and when the limits are $\pm(\epsilon-i)$ the *minor standstill*. The Moon, it is true, in no sense stands still, but for about a year the limiting declinations do not vary by more than 20 arc minutes, so that for month after month the Moon's declination goes through almost the same cycle.

But there are small variations in this cycle produced by the perturbation. The scale of Fig. 2.2 is much too small to show this effect. It is best seen by looking at what happened at a typical standstill, that of 1969. Fig. 2.3 may be looked on as an enlargement of the upper limit line at Q of Fig. 2.2. But we have, as it were, folded Fig. 2.2 about its horizontal axis so that the negative values can also be shown in Fig. 2.3, in which the filled rings show the monthly maximum positive declinations and the open rings the negative. For example, early in November 1968 the declination rose to $+28°\ 33'$ and 2 weeks later it had fallen to $-28°\ 30'$. The figure shows how the limits are subject to a wobble of amplitude Δ equal to about 9 arc minutes and a period of 173·3 days.

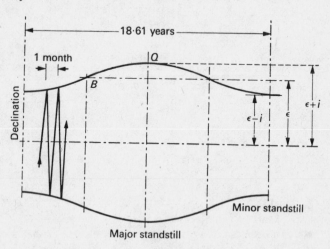

FIG. 2.2. The limits of the Moon's declination throughout one revolution of the line of nodes. The perturbation cycle is too small to show on this scale, but see Fig. 2.3 for detail at Q.

The danger times are shown in Fig. 2.3 and are marked 'ecliptic limits'. It is seen how they occur when the oscillation is a maximum. As Tycho pointed out, the Sun and the Moon are then in conjunction, which is the time of eclipses. The times of full and new Moon are shown along the top of the figure by open and filled rings. An outer ring has been added when an eclipse actually occurred. It will be seen how eclipses happen only inside the danger times. For example, the full Moon on 2 April 1969 was just outside the limit and was not eclipsed.

The exact time the Sun takes to traverse the danger arcs is discussed in standard textbooks. We can think of it as a period of about 3 weeks. For our present purpose the important thing is that it happens when the perturbation is a maximum. If Megalithic man could detect the perturbation and knew its period he would be in a position to predict eclipses. We shall see that the sites at Temple Wood and Mid Clyth demonstrate in considerable detail how he actually used this method. Had one or two more stones been removed from these sites we should have been left guessing.

2.4. It ought to be mentioned that the interval from one new Moon to the next has a *mean* value of 29·53 days, called the *synodic month*. The *tropical month*, or the time it takes the Moon to make a circuit of the heavens relative to ♈, has a mean value of 27·32 days. These periods are different because, while the Moon is making its circuit, the Sun has advanced, and the Moon

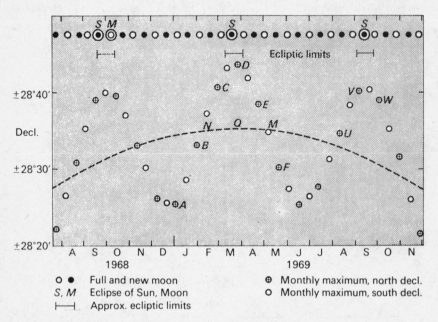

FIG. 2.3. Declination maxima (north and south) at the 1969 standstill.

needs the extra two days to catch up so that there can be another new Moon. The mean interval from one declination maximum to the next is the *tropical month* of 27·32 days. (See Appendix A.)

2.5. Let us now consider what an observer sees, or thinks he sees. If we imagine that we impose on the *whole* Universe a rotation equal and opposite to that of the Earth on its axis in Fig. 2.1, we bring the Earth to rest, but the celestial sphere, previously assumed stationary, now rotates. This is exactly what our senses tell us is happening when we look at the heavens. We want to assume the Earth stationary.

In Fig. 2.4 we have drawn the Earth large so that we can represent the celestial sphere centred on an observer supposed to be at *O*. Any slight differences produced in the appearance of the heavens when viewed from *O* instead of, as in Fig. 2.1, the Earth's centre are known as parallax corrections and can *for the moment* be ignored. Thus we use Fig. 2.1 or Fig. 2.4 according to our requirements. We see the plane of the observer's horizon *AWB* resting on the surface of the Earth at O. The points A, B, W, and E are the south, north, west, and east points on the horizon. Z is his zenith. OP is parallel to the Earth's axis and so P is the pole of the equator on the celestial sphere. The meridian is the plane $BPZTA$. At the equinoxes, when the Sun has zero

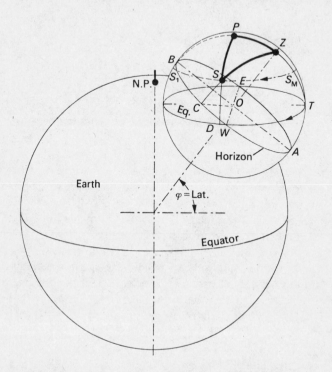

Fig. 2.4. The celestial sphere for an observer at O on the Earth's surface. $WCBA$ is the plane of the horizon, Z is the zenith, and the plane of the meridian is $BPZTA$. A star travels along the dotted small circle to set at S_1.

SD is the declination δ, $\therefore PS = 90° - \delta$ = polar distance.
SC is the altitude h, $\therefore ZS = 90° - h$ = zenith distance.
TZ is the latitude ϕ, $\therefore PZ = 90° - \phi$ = colatitude.
TD or $\angle SPZ$ = hour angle.
BC or $\angle PZS$ = 360° − azimuth.

declination, it rises at E and appears to move along the equator to transit the meridian at T and set at W. Remember that now it is the celestial sphere with all the heavenly bodies that is supposed to rotate about OP, as in fact to the observer it seems to do. A star S (or the Sun or Moon) with declination DS moves along the 'small circle' shown dotted, and crosses the meridian at S_M to set at S_1. When it is at S its altitude is CS. In this book we use the convention that azimuth is measured from the north point B round the horizon in a clockwise direction, so that the azimuth of the star S, which is the same thing as the azimuth of OC, is $360° - \angle COB$. Note that the angle COB is the same thing as the angle SZP. The observer's latitude ϕ is ZT, and so $PZ = 90° - \phi = $ colatitude.

It will be noticed that all the quantities we require can be expressed in terms of the sides and angles of the spherical triangle SPZ, which is often called the astronomical triangle. Thus

$$PS = 90° - \delta = \text{polar distance of } S,$$
$$PZ = 90° - \phi = \text{colatitude},$$
$$SZ = 90° - h = \text{zenith distance of } S,$$

where δ is the declination of S, h is its altitude, and ϕ is the latitude of the observer. The angle PZS tells us the azimuth of S, and the angle ZPS is the *hour angle*, i.e. angle between the observer's meridian and the meridian through the star. The hour angle is measured by the time that has elapsed since the star S was on the observer's meridian. If we are given any three of these five angles the other two can be found by 'solving the triangle' by standard trigonometrical formulae to be found in any textbook dealing with spherical trigonometry. The two formulae we shall need will be found in § 2.11.

While the reader may not want to master the spherical triangle and its numerous applications, it is desirable to be clear about the two presentations of the celestial sphere so that the movements of the Sun and the Moon shown in Fig. 2.1 can be translated by means of Fig. 2.4 into what happens in the observer's sky.

2.6. As I write this (1969) the Moon is coming through a major standstill. One cannot fail to be surprised to see it set and rise almost in the north. A fortnight later one is again surprised to see how far south are the rising and setting points and how very low it is at transit. The further north one goes the more pronounced are these phenomena, until in Shetland the Moon at its furthest north is almost circumpolar. In Megalithic times, because of the greater obliquity, it would have been possible to see the Moon actually circumpolar from the high ground in the most northerly part of the islands. This in itself would have drawn attention to the 18·6-year cycle.

Today in latitude 55° N the Moon is below the horizon for only some $4\frac{1}{2}$ hours for a few nights each month at the time of a major standstill. This means that at the time of a midwinter full Moon the Moon rises before the Sun sets and is still high in the sky when the sun rises. So at these times just when sunlight is scarcest there is bright moonlight all night when the Moon is full or nearly full. It is difficult for the present generation to realize how important this kind of thing must have been for a people who had, by modern standards, no artificial illumination. The writer well remembers the time when the only light available for driving at night was provided by carriage-lamps, each of which held one candle, sold as 'carriage moons'. Moonlight was in fact important in country districts for getting about until well into the present century. During the Second World War some societies took the precaution of arranging their winter meetings near to the time of full Moon.

The importance to Megalithic people of the Moon for illumination in the winter and for tidal prediction evidently caused them to make a study of its movements. The 18·6-year cycle would obtrude itself, if in fact it had not been recognized from time immemorial. Analogy with a probably earlier study of the solstices would suggest the use of a horizon mark with a back-sight. Once this technique was applied seriously the irregularities at the standstills would have become apparent. There was a real difficulty here, as we shall see shortly, but sooner or later someone noticed that eclipses happened at the new or full Moon nearest to the date when the Moon attained its absolute extreme positions. This would inspire an examination of the wobble, which was to form such an important study at the lunar observatories. One can think of no way in which this wobble could have been detected by these people except by careful observations made at one of the standstills.

2.7. The theory of the motion of the Moon is a highly complex subject, which has occupied the attention of some of our best mathematicians for a large part of their lives. Here we are not interested in the hundreds of small terms which have to be included to obtain the accuracy demanded by modern astronomy. From what has been said earlier we see that the apparent movement in declination can be broadly described by saying it consists of three cyclical components. There is a large roughly sinusoidal component with a mean period of 27·32 days and an amplitude controlled by the sinusoidal limits as shown in Fig. 2.2. These limits have a period of 18·61 years and an amplitude of $i = 5° 8' 43''$. Superimposed on this long-period component there is the small perturbation of period 173·3 days and an amplitude not quite constant, but never getting very far from 9 arc minutes.

Near a standstill it is sufficient to consider that these three components are additive. Let us write any one of them as $y = g \cos 2\pi t/P$, where t is the time in days from the time of the maximum of the component considered, P is the period, and g is the amplitude. The declination deficiency, or the amount by which the component falls below its maximum g, is $y = g - g \cos 2\pi t/P$, which can be written $2g \sin^2(\pi t/P)$. Provided the time t is small compared to the period, we can replace the sine by the angle, so that the declination deficiency can be written $2g\pi^2 t^2/P^2$, or more simply kt^2, where $k = 2g\pi^2/P^2$.

What we are doing is to replace the top of a component by a simple parabola

$$y = kt^2. \tag{2.2}$$

With t expressed in days and y in arc minutes the values of k for the three components are:

27·32-day component at major standstill,	$g = \epsilon + i$,	$k_1 = 46\cdot0$,
27·32-day component at minor standstill,	$g = \epsilon - i$,	$k_2 = 30\cdot0$,
18·61-year component,	$g = i$,	$k_3 = 0\cdot000132$,
173·3-day component, amplitude $\Delta = 8'\cdot7$,	$g = 8'\cdot7$,	$k_4 = 0\cdot0057$.

It may be noted here that the value 27·32 days is a mean, which remains constant from century to century, but individual values may vary considerably.

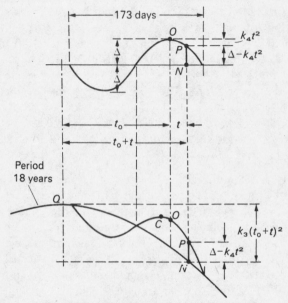

FIG. 2.5. Displacement of the maximum.

For an understanding of what comes in later chapters it is desirable to be quite clear about the above. As an example, suppose that the lunar declination attains its maximum value for the month at midnight. Then half a day later it will have fallen by $46\cdot5 \times (\frac{1}{2})^2$, or about $11'\cdot6$. By the following midnight the deficiency will be $46'\cdot5$, and a day later still it will be four times as much. By comparison, note how slowly the 18-year component falls: after 100 days only $0\cdot000132 \times 100^2$ or $1'\cdot32$.

2.8. As another example of the use of the expressions for the declination deficiencies let us examine the distortion produced on the 173-day perturbation cycle when it is superimposed on the long 18-year cycle. At the top of Fig. 2.5 we see the undisturbed wave. At a time t after its maximum O it has fallen from Δ to $\Delta - k_4 t^2$. Below we see it added to the 18-year oscillation, the maximum Q of which has happened t_0 earlier. At time t the combined curve will be below Q by $k_3(t_0+t)^2-(\Delta-k_4 t^2)$. Differentiating this to find the time of the highest point C yields

$$t_{max} = -k_3 t_0/(k_3+k_4) = -0.022\,t_0. \tag{2.3}$$

This is negative, showing that C is earlier than O. It will be evident that the time interval between any two not necessarily successive maxima will be reduced by 2·2 per cent; no matter if the observers found a method of determining the period by exact observation of the maxima, it would be subject to this error. It is true that the error in the period as determined from the minima is of opposite sign, but we do not know if they understood this.

The above stricture does not apply if the two maxima belonged to different

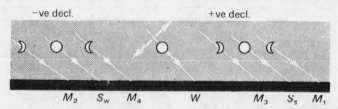

FIG. 2.6. The western sky (see also Thom 1967, Fig. 3.2).

standstills, a method that was possible (and accurate) if the number of intermediate maxima was known. This was possible if an approximate value of the period was known, or if careful track had been kept of the intervening eclipses.

2.9. It is desirable to have a clear idea of the Moon's apparent movements in the sky. We shall accordingly explain these again without any reference to the causes. The reader can then relate these movements to what has been said before.

Fig. 2.6 shows the western sky. The midsummer Sun sets in the north-west at S_s, the equinoctial Sun sets in the west at W, and the midwinter Sun sets in the south-west at S_w. Thus in a year the setting point oscillates from S_s to S_w and back again. Similarly the setting point of the Moon oscillates, but in a month instead of a year. Whereas S_s and S_w are fixed points, the limits of the Moon's oscillation are not fixed, but can vary between fixed limits. When the Moon is seen to set in its extreme northern position M_1, 2 weeks later it will set in its extreme southern position M_2. These limits M_1 and M_2 will gradually narrow until after 9 years they have become M_3 and M_4. After 18·6 years the setting points will again be oscillating between M_1 and M_2.

We associate M_1 and M_2 with what we propose to call the major standstill because for several months there is but little change in the limits. For the same reason the time when the limits are stationary at M_3 and M_4 will be called the minor standstill.

The above is the broad picture; but, if we have erected foresights of sufficient accuracy, we shall find that the limits are subject to another oscillation of small amplitude and period 173 days. This small oscillation is associated with eclipses in such a way that they can happen only when the oscillation is making its greatest contribution to the limits existing at the time. This does not mean that eclipses happen only when the Moon is reaching M_1 or M_2. M_1 and M_2 are the limits of the 18-year period. Eclipses can happen near any maximum of the 173-day oscillation.

The above way of looking at the matter may lead to confusion if we fall into the trap of arguing that, since eclipses happen when the Moon is near the ecliptic and since the Sun is always on the ecliptic, eclipses cannot happen when the Moon is far to the right of S_S, e.g. at M_1. But when the Moon sets at M_1, a few days later its declination will have decreased and an eclipse may, and in fact probably will, take place if the small oscillation is at a maximum. Remember that the small oscillation is going on all the time, but it could have been visible to Megalithic man at the standstills only.

2.10. Having mastered the above, the reader must face up to another difficulty that has been glossed over. The declination of the Moon changes so fast that, at a particular lunation, it may come up to its maximum and again decrease between two observations, which are of necessity always separated by about a day. This in fact is a real difficulty, probably the greatest which Megalithic man encountered in his study of the perturbation. The declination deficiency in 12 hours at a particular lunation may be as large as or slightly larger than the perturbation being studied. Considering the limitations under which these people worked, the method they evolved to overcome this difficulty was indeed a triumph. Unfortunately I have so far found no method of explaining it without using a modicum of mathematics. In Chapter 8 an exposition will be given using only what today must be considered elementary mathematics. When the sites are being described an attempt will be made to show how the idea developed as the builders sought greater and greater accuracy. We shall never know what genius was responsible for the final step, we may never know where he lived, but we do know that it is only in Caithness that the remains are such as to demonstrate clearly the working of the method.

2.11. Some necessary formulae

The trigonometry of the spherical triangle SPZ provides the two formulae

$$\cot \text{Az.} = \sin \phi \cot H - \cos \phi \tan \delta / \sin H, \tag{2.4}$$

$$\sin \delta = \sin \phi \sin h + \cos \phi \cos h \cos \text{Az.} \tag{2.5}$$

The first is used for finding the Sun's azimuth when its hour angle H and its declination δ are given. Its use is described in Appendix B. The second formula is used for calculating the declination of a point from its azimuth and altitude. In both ϕ is the latitude.

In analysing some of the sites we shall need to find the change in declination produced by unit change in altitude. We get this by differentiating (2.5) to obtain

$$d\delta/dh = \sin\phi \cos h/\cos\delta - \cos\phi \sin h \cos \text{Az.}/\cos\delta. \tag{2.6}$$

The second term is usually negligible and $\cos h$ is practically unity. Similarly for the effect of azimuth we have

$$d\delta/d\text{Az.} = -\cos\phi \cos h \sin \text{Az.}/\cos\delta. \tag{2.7}$$

Normally these differential formulae are sufficient to enable us to find the change in declination produced by a small change in the observer's position, but cases can, and do, arise where they are insufficient. For example, suppose that the foresight is a V notch in the horizon produced by the slopes of two hills, one slope running behind the other. The difference in distance to the two slopes may be such that a change in the observer's position produces what is really a different foresight. It is then best to determine the altitude and azimuth of the foresight from two or more points on the line of the oberver's movement and to compute the declination for each. The effective distance to the apparent foresight can, if required, be then computed. This method was used at Temple Wood and Mid Clyth.

3

REFRACTION AND PARALLAX

3.1. IN later chapters a number of horizon profiles are given. Many of these have been measured by theodolite by the methods described in Appendix B, but others are the result of calculation using the largest scale Ordnance Survey available with contours. Those measured are plotted straight from the measurements and so represent day-time conditions, but for the calculated profiles an attempt has been made to show night-time conditions. The object of this chapter is to discuss the necessary corrections to the profile altitudes so that they can be used to find declinations. These corrections are by no means negligible: if they were not made, any analysis of the lunar declinations obtained would be meaningless. An example of the error which can arise is to be seen in Fig. 9.2.

3.2. Refraction

Under ordinary circumstances the air density decreases with height. This causes a ray of light to bend so that it is concave towards the ground. The apparent increase in the (angular) altitude of a distant object thereby produced is known as *terrestrial refraction* when the object is on the Earth, or *astronomical refraction* when the object is a celestial body.

In Fig. 3.1 a ray of light coming from a star along the line SMO grazes the mountain top M and reaches the observer at O. To him it appears to have come from S_a. Were there no atmosphere the star would be seen along the straight line OS_1. The line OW, the horizontal, is tangent at O, but the height of the mountain MN is measured from the Earth's surface ON, which is curved with radius ρ. Knowing ρ, the height of the mountain MN, and its distance L, we can calculate the geometrical altitude of M, namely θ. The observer measures with his theodolite not θ but h, which is greater than θ by the terrestrial refraction T.

The true altitude of the star is marked h_t, but its apparent altitude is of course the same as that of M, namely h. Let R and T denote astronomical and terrestrial refraction. These are marked on the figure, showing that

$$h = h_t + R = \theta + T,$$

from which

$$h_t = h - R = \theta + T - R. \tag{3.1}$$

This gives h_t, from which, with the azimuth and latitude, the declination may be calculated; but if we are dealing with the Sun or the Moon a further correction for parallax must be applied. When finding h_t by this method we use values of T and R estimated for the hours of darkness, or in the case of the Sun for the time of sunset. But if h has been measured by theodolite

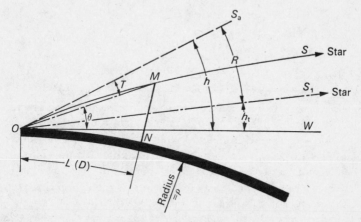

FIG. 3.1. The refracted ray.

during the day then ideally we proceed thus. Designate day and night values by subscripts d and n. Then

$$h_n = \theta + T_n \quad \text{and} \quad h_d = \theta + T_d,$$

from which

$$h_n = h_d + T_n - T_d. \tag{3.2}$$

But, as the site is supposed to have been used at night, the true altitude is

$$h_t = h_n - R_n = h_d - R_n + (T_n - T_d). \tag{3.3}$$

Thus having measured h_d we correct it for night-time astronomical re-fraction and the difference between day and night terrestrial refraction. The last term is appreciable only when the distance L to the horizon is greater than 5–10 miles.

3.3. Terrestrial refraction

The refraction that is experienced by a horizontal ray between two terrestrial points is subject to large and to a great extent unpredictable variations from the mean. It is affected by weather, wind, time of day, and local terrain. In a situation that might be considered as being typical of a Megalithic site the author took over 500 refraction measurements in a series extending over several years. The altitudes of a number of hill and mountain peaks and of two nearer marks were measured in all possible conditions of weather, time of day, wind, and cloud. The refraction was expressed as

$$T'' = KLP/t^2,\qquad\qquad(3.4)$$

where T'' = refraction (arc seconds),

P = barometric pressure (inches of mercury),

t = temperature (°R, i.e. °F+460),

L = length of the ray (feet),

K = refraction constant.

For details of how K is affected by temperature gradient, wind, cloud, etc. reference must be made to the original paper (Thom 1958). Here we are concerned mainly with the behaviour of the mean value of K. The raw results uncorrected for the effects of wind and temperature gradient are very scattered. Values of K ranged from 5 to 13, but when means were taken for various times of day (expressed as a fraction of the interval from noon to sunset) a definite result emerged. In Fig. 3.2 each point is the mean of n observations, where n is the number written at the bottom of the figure. It is seen that *on the average* the lowest refraction occurs in the early afternoon in both summer and winter, and the highest occurs after sunset. Some ninety measurements were also made to two distant lighthouses, from shortly before dark to midnight and also before dawn. These results were scattered from $7\frac{1}{2}$ to 15 and showed a mean of about 11.

When in the evening the ground cools by radiation to a clear sky the lower layers of air cool first. This means that the normal fall of air density with height is enhanced, and so, since it is the density gradient that bends the ray, the refraction is increased. It should be remembered that an alteration in the ray curvature in the neighbourhood of a point Q has an effect on refraction that is proportional to the distance of Q from the *far* end of the line. It follows that it is the terrain near the observer that has the greatest effect, the more so as that end of the line will be low and near the ground. The high values found for the lighthouses above were probably not produced by the 15–20 miles of the ray that ran over the sea at the far end, but by the few miles of the near end where the ray was near the ground.

3.4. When calculating the apparent altitude of a point like M (Fig. 3.1) from its distance and height, allowance must be made for curvature of the Earth's surface. This curvature is much greater than the curvature of the light ray produced by refraction.

Taking into account the azimuth of the ray and the latitude, one can calculate the curvature of the surface of the spheroid that geodetists consider best fits the geoid or actual shape of a level surface on the Earth. This was done for the rays used in the study of refraction discussed in § 3.3, but for our present purpose it is sufficient to use a mean radius of curvature $\rho = 21 \times 10^6$ feet. In Fig. 3.1 the distance of N below the plane OW is, from the geometry of the circle, $L^2/2\rho$. The corresponding drop in the apparent altitude of M is $L/2\rho$ radians.

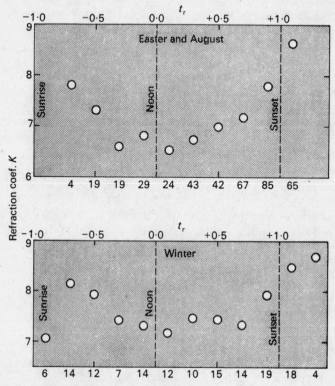

FIG. 3.2. Effect of time of day on refraction,

where $t_r = (t_o - t_n)/(t_s - t_n)$,

t_o = time of observation,

t_n = time of local apparent noon,

t_s = time of sunset.

Each ring is the mean of n observations, where n is the number written below the ring.

Put $H = H_M - H_O$, where H_M and H_O are the heights in feet of M and the observer O above Ordnance Datum. Then the apparent altitude of M is, in radians,

$$h = H/L - L/2\rho + T. \tag{3.5}$$

To obtain a working formula we take the refraction T from (3.4), write the distance as D miles, and adopt a mean pressure of 29·9 inches. The altitude in arc minutes then becomes

$$h = 0.651\, H/D - 0.432\, D + 2631\, KD/t^2. \tag{3.6}$$

When we wish to calculate the apparent altitude of a point after dark we can use

$$h = 0.651\,H/D - 0.31\,D, \tag{3.7}$$

which corresponds to $K = 12$ and a temperature of 45 °F.

During the day the temperature will be higher and K will be lower, giving a numerically higher second term. Reasonably good agreement between measured and calculated altitudes will be found by using

$$h = 0.651\,H/D - 0.36\,D. \tag{3.8}$$

The second term becomes important only when the ray is long. On the other hand, the contours on the Ordnance Survey are not at a close enough interval to permit of accuracy in short distances.

When it is considered desirable to take account of the last term in (3.3) we may proceed thus. Suppose that the profile is measured with a temperature of t_0, the estimated refraction coefficient being K_0. For the time when the site was used, probably at night, the estimated values are t_n and K_n. Then

$$T_n = T_0 + (t_n - t_0)\,\partial T/\partial t + (K_n - K_0)\,\partial T/\partial K.$$

This correction is usually small and is normally swamped by other uncertainties, but when it is desired to use it a simplified form can be deduced using (3.4):

$$T_n - T_0 = 0.01\,D(K_n - K_0) - 0.0003\,D(t_n - t_0). \tag{3.9}$$

This is in arc minutes, D being the length of the ray in miles.

3.5. Dip of the horizon

The angular depression of the apparent sea horizon is known as *dip*. We cannot construct a profile involving the sea unless we know the magnitude of this angle. When the altitude (or negative dip) of the sea horizon has been measured it may be necessary to estimate how much it is likely to be affected by the change of refraction from day-time when it was measured, to night-time when Megalithic man used the site.

In Fig. 3.3 the observer at A, at a height H feet above sea level, sees the horizon in the apparent direction AE, tangent at A to the light ray BA. At B this ray and the surface of the sea have a common tangent BE. It is not difficult to show that

$$\text{Dip} = \sqrt{\{2H(1/\rho - 1/\sigma)\}}, \tag{3.10}$$

where ρ and σ are the radii of curvature of the Earth's surface and of the ray. $\rho = 21 \times 10^6$ ft and $1/\sigma =$ twice the refraction (radians) per foot. Taking the refraction from (3.4) with 29.9 in pressure and 45 °F we obtain

$$\text{Dip} = 1.061\sqrt{H}\sqrt{(1 - 0.0238\,K)} \text{ arc minutes.} \tag{3.11}$$

The *Nautical Almanac* gives for the dip $0.97\sqrt{H}$, a value that can be obtained by putting $K = 6.9$ in (3.11). But if we are constructing a profile from the Ordnance Survey as it will appear after dark, and it is appropriate to use a high value of refraction, then to be consistent we ought to use a low value of dip; e.g. if we are using $K = 12$ and put this value in (3.11) we find that the dip is about $0.90\sqrt{H}$.

A criticism of these formulae is that they assume a uniform curvature of the ray throughout its length. When a high value of the refraction constant K is found experimentally, it almost certainly indicates, at least on a long ray,

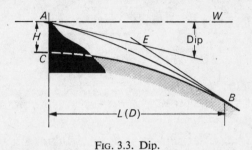

FIG. 3.3. Dip.

that there is a higher curvature at the near end of the ray. This would mean that K depends on the length of the ray. But, in view of the uncertainties that must exist, it seems better at present to keep the simpler form suggested. Enough is known to show that for long distances and low altitudes a daylight measurement does not in itself give the answer. One of the objects of this chapter has been to show how to adjust such measurements so that the night-time altitudes may be *estimated*.

3.6. Astronomical refraction

We have seen that terrestrial refraction is subject to large unpredictable variations. In so far as the astronomical ray and the terrestrial ray are identical from M to O (Fig. 3.1), astronomical refraction is subject to the same vagaries. For very low and negative altitudes the ray may still be under the influence of weather conditions at low heights for a long distance beyond M. Consequently it is not surprising that authorities differ by several per cent in their values of astronomical refraction at low altitudes. But they differ still more widely as to the effect of temperature. Values of the decrease in refraction produced by a temperature increase of 1 °F as given by different writers vary between 5″ and 8″ at zero apparent altitude.

Table 3.1 shows the values that have been used for the lunar lines in this book. The effect of atmospheric pressure is not serious and 29·9 in mercury has been assumed at sea-level.

A mean temperature of 45 °F has been used. It is perhaps arguable that a higher value should be used for the south declinations since these may have been used more often in summer, but this refinement does not seem necessary unless we can obtain profiles of greater accuracy.

Table 3.1. *Astronomical refraction at* 29·9 inHg *and* 45 °F *as a function of apparent altitude*

App. alt.	Refr. R	Decrease per °F	App. alt.	Refr. R	Decrease per °F	App. alt.	Refr. R	Decrease per °F
−20′	40′.	?	1° 00′	24′·5	0·055	2° 30′	16′·2	0·033
0	34·8	0·10	1 20	22·1	0·048	3 00	14·4	0·028
+20	30·6	0·08	1 40	20·1	0·043	4 00	11·8	0·023
+40	27·2	0·065	2 00	18·3	0·038	5 00	9·9	0·019

3.7. Parallax

Relative to the distance to the Moon the Earth is a large body. It follows that the position of the observer on the Earth affects the direction in which he sees the Moon. To reduce an observed position of the Moon to what it would have been if the observation had been made at the Earth's centre, the observed altitude must be decreased by the refraction and increased by the parallax correction. The azimuth is not affected. The correction for parallax is greatest when the Moon is on the horizon, and is then known as horizontal parallax (p). At an altitude h the correction becomes $p \cos h$, which is, as it obviously should be, zero in the zenith.

Parallax and refraction have this in common. The effect on the observed declination of, for example, the Sun is of the same sign algebraically whether the Sun is in its north position (summer) or in its south position (winter). This means that the effect on the *numerical* value of the declinations is of opposite sign. If that in the north is increased that in the south is decreased. The mean value is unaffected. This applies to both the Sun and the Moon in their extreme positions and makes possible the kind of analysis of observed declinations to be given later. But at the same time it makes it difficult to separate the effects of refraction and parallax.

The horizontal parallax is inversely proportional to the distance to the Moon, and, since this distance is smallest when the Moon is at perigee, parallax is then greatest, being about 61′·5. At apogee p has fallen to about 53′·9. The mean value with respect to time is 57′ 3″. In revolving round the Earth it takes the Moon a mean time-interval of 27·55455 days from perigee to perigee. Hence in this period the parallax goes through one cycle between the limits just given. This period is not greatly different from the tropical month of 27·32159 days, which is the mean interval from one declination maximum to the next. We shall in Chapter 7 carefully consider the effect of these periods being so close. Suffice it to say here that it puts a lower limit on our estimate of the length of time spent on the erection of the observatories. On the other hand, in the very unlikely eventuality that archaeologists assured us that a given site had been occupied only for a lesser period, it might be possible to say just when these years were.

Parallax, like refraction, must have produced anomalous effects on Megalithic man's observations that he would have found difficult to explain, but we shall show that, if he really tried, his observatories were capable of giving results that might have had far-reaching effects on his knowledge and philosophy.

4

SOLSTITIAL SITES

4.1. THERE are many places in Britain where we find a Megalithic indication of the rising or setting point of the Sun at the summer or winter solstice, but only a few of these are today accurate enough or complete enough to enable us to deduce with any precision the Sun's solstitial declination, i.e. the obliquity of the ecliptic (ϵ). Some may have had an artificial foresight of perishable material, or, as at Sornach Coir Fhinn (Thom 1967, fig. 11.7), the foresight may have consisted of a stone structure, now ruinous, on a ridge forming the skyline. But only those that made use of a mountain or hill profile as a foresight provide the kind of accuracy we are seeking here. Ideally for this examination all sites used should be of the same date. By using sites in the same district we hope that this condition is fulfilled with sufficient accuracy.

We can, with a theodolite and an accurate watch, measure up these profiles, but when we come to deduce the declination we are faced with the difficulty that we cannot estimate the refraction that existed when Megalithic man made use of the site. It may be true that mean refraction under similar meteorological conditions has not changed much, but the weather has, and so the corrections for temperature and barometric pressure in Megalithic times are somewhat uncertain.

When I first wrote on this subject (Thom 1954) I pointed out that if we could find accurate foresights for all four cases (midsummer and midwinter, rising and setting) we could to some extent eliminate the effects of refraction, and so make an accurate determination of the obliquity of the ecliptic and therefore an estimate of the date of erection. The theory behind this statement will be given and it will be illustrated by a set of foresights in Argyllshire. One of these is somewhat uncertain, but this by no means invalidates the conclusions.

4.2. Of the solstitial sites known to the author the most important are at Ballochroy and Kintraw. These will now be described. Sites are classified according to district. Thus A 4 means Argyllshire, Kintyre. A list of the districts with classification letter and number is given on p. 124.

Ballochroy, A 4/4, NR 730524

A plan of Ballochroy will be found in the lower half of Fig. 4.1. The flat face of the centre menhir indicates exactly Corra Bheinn, the most northerly peak in the Paps of Jura. The inset (*b*) shows how the upper limb of the Sun setting at midsummer in Megalithic times just grazed the top of the slope as viewed from S_1. Viewed from the kist the limb would graze the lower slopes. Looking along the line $S_1 S_2 S_3$ to the kist one sees the island of Cara. The inset (*a*) shows how the midwinter setting Sun just grazed the end of Cara.

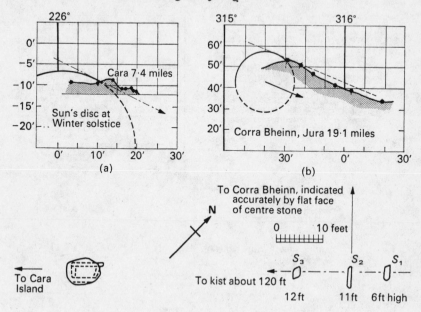

(a) (b)

FIG. 4.1. Ballochroy, A 4/4, NR 730524 (55° 42′ 44″, 5° 36′ 45″), showing (*a*) the midwinter Sun setting over Cara Island as seen from the stones; (*b*) the midsummer setting Sun as seen from stone S_1. From the kist the profile azimuths are 5′ greater.

Kintraw, A 2/5, NM 830050

Fig. 4.2 shows the setting midwinter Sun as seen from Kintraw *c.* 1700 B.C. After the Sun had vanished behind Beinn Shiantaidh a minute portion of the luminous disc would reappear momentarily in the col. The observer would seek by rapid movement across the line of sight to reduce the brilliant light to a point while the limb slid past the bottom of the notch. An alternative method would make use of a row of observers. To those at the left the Sun would not reappear at all. The first man along the line to see the twinkle of light would be in the correct position, which would immediately be marked by a stake. If this process were repeated on several evenings around the time of the solstice the stake position would move first towards the right and then towards the left. The extreme right position would mark the day of the solstice.

To understand how accurate this technique can be (were it not bedevilled by refraction changes from evening to evening) one can look at the green flash. When the Sun sinks behind a clean-cut horizon in a clear sky the last visible part of the disc to be seen is very small and is usually a bright emerald green. If we assume its width to be 2 arc minutes, and it is perhaps less, the depth (the sagitta) is $(1 \times 1)/32$ minutes, or about 2 arc seconds. In the clearer

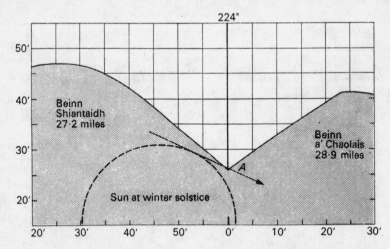

FIG. 4.2. Midwinter sunset from Kintraw, A 2/5, NM 830050 (Lat. 56° 11'·3).

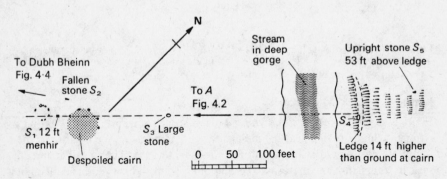

FIG. 4.3. Remains at Kintraw, Argyll, A 2/5, NM 830050.

skies of Megalithic times the observers would see and perhaps use the green flash as a criterion that they were in the correct position. They could thus obtain an accuracy of a few seconds. During the first 24 hours after the instant of the solstice the sun's declination decreases numerically by about 12 seconds. After a further 24 hours the decrease is about four times as great, progressing steadily as the square of the interval (see § 2.7). At Kintraw 12 arc seconds of declination correspond to about 19 feet sideways movement. It thus appears that if refraction remained constant for a few evenings the observers had to hand a method of obtaining by direct observation the day of the solstice (see Thom 1967, p. 117).

Attention was drawn in 1954 (Thom) to the accuracy of the Kintraw site, but at that time there was an unresolved difficulty. The site is situated on a small plateau on the otherwise very steep hillside where the road from Loch Craignish winds up to the Bealach Mor (the Big Pass) and so to Kilmartin and Lochgilphead. From ground level on the plateau a nearby ridge hides the

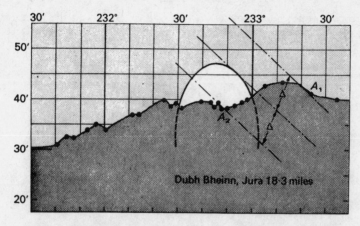

FIG. 4.4. Kintraw, A 2/5. Moon setting on Jura hills with declination
$= -(\epsilon - i)$ as seen from the cairn.

Paps and so the phenomenon of the Sun reappearing would not be visible. To see the col one must move to the right, when the azimuth of the col is too low to give the solstice, or climb some structure such as the cairn, which is in the correct position. How did the builders know where to place the cairn when they could not see the col from ground level? The answer, obvious now, is that they first established a position on the steep hillside to the north of the plateau. But a deep almost impassable gorge with a stream in the bottom comes between the plateau and the hillside. Also the hillside is much too steep to permit of the rapid sideways movement necessary when observing, and below is the dangerous gorge. But if anyone cares to climb up from the bridge and along above the gorge to the hillside he will be rewarded by finding himself on a little platform like a short stretch of narrow road cut into the hillside. This ledge, although only some 14 feet above the ground level at the cairn, is not immediately obvious from the main site. Lying on the edge of the ledge is a large stone, which may have been upright, and from here the col appears behind the menhir. On the line, or nearly on the line, there is on the low part of the plateau another boulder.

The original work must have been done on the platform. It would have been very easy to miss the phenomenon. An obvious precaution was to have a man stationed higher up to give warning that the limb was coming into view. Mr. R. L. Merritt drew my attention to another stone 100 feet up the slope and so 53 feet above the platform. This stone is about 2½ feet high and might be said to be orientated correctly. Perhaps the warning was given from this position.

Two other less impressive sites will now be described.

East Loch Tarbert, Jura, A 6/5, NR 609822

There are two stones here some 600 yards apart. The line to the west apparently gives a calendar declination (Thom 1967). The west stone is some

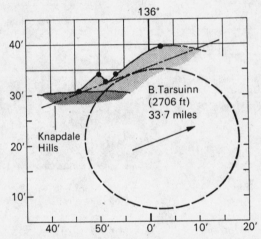

FIG. 4.5. Midwinter Sun rising behind B. Tarsuinn, Arran, as seen from west stone, E. Loch Tarbert, Jura.

10 feet high × 21 in × 8 in and is orientated 150°±10°. The other is over 6 feet high × 17 in × 6 in, orientated 358°±3°. From the large west stone Beinn Tarsuinn, Arran, 2706 feet, just shows above the Knapdale hills. The measured profile is shown in Fig. 4.5. Two definite notches are seen, but the declinations are identical. In view of the fact that the orientation is roughly right this can be accepted as a solstitial site for the midwinter rising Sun.

Peninver, Kintyre, A 4/10, NR 761254

This stone is 8 or 9 feet high and so projects above the modern wall that abuts on it on both sides. It is not orientated on the (assumed) foresight, which in any case it could not differentiate from the other notches in the mountain ridge (Fig. 4.6) that runs from Suidhe Fergus to the Peaks of the Castles in Arran. It may be that it is by chance that the notch A shows so closely the rising of the upper limb of the Sun on Midsummer Day. This site has been retained because it completes the set and so permits the method of analysis to be demonstrated.

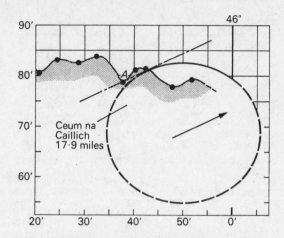

FIG. 4.6. Peninver, Kintyre. Midsummer Sun rising
on Ceum na Caillich, Arran.

4.3. Finding the obliquity of the ecliptic

It may be argued that in this paragraph the work has been unnecessarily complicated by the inclusion of various small terms, but in § 7.3 it will appear that the value of ϵ that we obtain has an important bearing on our main subject. Consequently every effort has been made to get the best value possible from the material available at the date of writing. There are, however, anomalous effects coming in due to the unknown and unpredictable nature of refraction. In an attempt to minimize some of these effects several of the profiles have been measured on different days, and wherever possible checks have been obtained by calculating the apparent altitudes of the peaks from the Ordnance Survey heights. Some further improvement could be obtained by making all the measurements at the time of sunset or sunrise.

Table 4.1 gives the azimuths and observed altitudes h_o of the assumed foresights. At Ballochroy the top of the Corra Bheinn slope as seen from the menhir S_1 and the lower slope as seen from the kist are both given (Fig. 4.1). At Tarbert, Jura (Fig. 4.5), only one point is given: the other lower point showed on calculation an identical declination. The values of h_o tabulated were measured at temperatures not very different from 60 °F. From h_o we now try to estimate what the true geocentric altitude would have been, e.g. at Ballochroy at sunset on Midsummer Day in Megalithic times, when the temperature is assumed to have been $60°+t$. There are four unknown values of t, summer and winter, morning and evening, and these unknowns t_1, t_2, etc. will remain in the expressions until they are eliminated algebraically.

Using (3.3) we have for the desired true altitude

$$h_t = h_o - R_n + (T_n - T_o) + p, \tag{4.1}$$

Table 4.1. *Finding* ϵ

		Peninver to Arran	Ballochroy kist to Corra B.	S_1 to Corra B.	Tarbert to B. Tarsuinn	Kintraw to Jura	Ballochroy to Cara Island
		Sum. morn.	Summer evening		Win. morn.	Winter evening	
Dist.	D (miles)	18	19	19	33	28	7
Lat.	ϕ	55° 28′·2	55° 42′·7	55° 42′·7	55° 58′·4	56° 11′·3	55° 42′·7
Az.	A	45 38	316 5	315 38	135 51	224 0	226 16
Alt.	h_o	1 19	40	52·3	32·5	26·1	−10·9
Refr.	R_{60}	21·5	26·3	24·5	27·5	28·3	35·5
Par.	p	0·1	0·1	0·1	0·1	0·1	0·1
	h_t	+57·6	+13·8	+27·9	+5·1	−2·1	−46·3
		Substitute above values of ϕ, A, and h_t in (2.5) and so find δ:					
Decl. δ		+24° 12′·7	+24° 9′·0	+24° 10′·2	−23° 35′·7	−23° 37′·7	−23° 36′·8
Semidiam.		15·9	15·9	15·9	16·2	16·2	16·2
	β	+23 56·8	+23 53·1	+23 54·3	−23 51·9	−23 53·9	−23 53·0
dR/dt		−0·048	−0·065	−0·058	−0·070	−0·075	−0·116
$0·0003 D$		+0·005	+0·006	+0·006	+0·010	+0·008	+0·002
Sum		−0·043	−0·059	−0·052	−0·060	−0·067	−0·114
$d\delta/dh$		0·903	0·904	0·904	0·905	0·906	0·905
b		0·039	0·053	0·047	0·054	0·060	0·103
B		+6′·8	mean = +3′·7		−1′·9	mean = −3′·5	
b		0·039	mean = 0·050		0·054	mean = 0·081	
B/b		+175	+74		−35	−43	
$1/b$		26	20		19	12	

$\Sigma|B/b| = 327$ $\Sigma[1/b] = 77$
$\Delta\epsilon = 2k\theta/77 + 327/77 = 0·026\, k\theta + 4′·25$

where p = Sun's horizontal parallax,

R_n = astronomical refraction at e.g. sunset = $R + t\, dR/dt$,

where R = refraction at 60 °F. In evaluating $(T_n - T_o)$ by (3.9) put $K_n = K_o$, since in all cases the ray runs over the sea for the important part of its length so that the rise in refraction at morning or evening may not take place. Thus (4.1) becomes

$$h_t = h_o - R + p - t(dR/dt + 0·0003\, D), \qquad (4.2)$$

D being the distance to the foresight in miles, and dR/dt obtainable from Table 3.1.

For the time being omit the term in t and calculate the declination by (2.5) as in Table 4.1. The semidiameters shown have been calculated from the elements of the Earth's orbit at about 1700 B.C. (Thom 1967). Applying these we obtain what we shall call β, or the first approximation to the declination. Bringing in the omitted term in t the final value of the declination becomes

$$\beta + kt(-dR/dt - 0·0003\, D)\, d\delta/dh, \qquad (4.3)$$

which we shall write $\beta + kbt$, where

$$b = (-dR/dt - 0·0003\, D)\, d\delta/dh. \qquad (4.4)$$

dδ/dh is found from (2.6) and dR/dt is from Table 3.1. The unknown k has been inserted so that in the end we have some idea of the error being introduced by uncertainties in the term in brackets.

Anyone is competent to guess the temperatures, summer and winter, morning and evening, which obtained in Megalithic times, and so to calculate a value of the declination, that is ϵ, from each column in Table 4.1. The mean could then be taken. The following analysis, however, in forming the mean formally eliminates to a great extent the unknown temperatures.

We can write the following four equations:

$$
\begin{aligned}
\text{summer morning} \quad & \epsilon = \beta_1 + kb_1 t_1, \\
\text{summer evening} \quad & \epsilon = \beta_2 + kb_2 t_2, \\
\text{winter morning} \quad & \epsilon = \beta_3 + kb_3 t_3, \\
\text{winter evening} \quad & \epsilon = \beta_4 + kb_4 t_4.
\end{aligned}
\tag{4.5}
$$

But there are five unknowns, namely ϵ, kt_1, kt_2, kt_3, and kt_4. For the necessary fifth equation probably the best alternative is to put $2\theta = (t_1+t_2)-(t_3+t_4)$, which in words means that θ is the difference between the averages of the summer and winter temperatures. We know that today θ is not far from 20°. We can now solve these five equations for ϵ and find

$$
\begin{aligned}
\epsilon &= (2k\theta+\beta_1/b_1+\beta_2/b_2-\beta_3/b_3-\beta_4/b_4)/(1/b_1+1/b_2+1/b_3+1/b_4) \\
&= (2k\theta+\textstyle\sum|\beta/b|)/\textstyle\sum(1/b).
\end{aligned}
\tag{4.6}
$$

Details are given in Table 4.1. To shorten the arithmetic we have written B for the excess of β over 23° 50′.

Substituting values we find

$$
\epsilon = 0\cdot026\,k\theta + 23° \, 54'\cdot25.
$$

θ is about 20° today, but if in Megalithic times the climate was more of a continental nature it might have then been larger. The values used for dR/dt may be in error. Accordingly in Table 4.2 the effect of using different values of θ and k is shown.

Table 4.2. *Effect of θ and k on ϵ and on the temperatures deduced from* Table 4.1

θ	20	25	Omit Peninver
k	1	1·5	$k=1$
$\epsilon = 23° \, 50' +$	4′·8	5′·2	4′·2
Temperature:			
Summer morning	8 °F	32 °F	—
Summer evening	81	80	69 °F
Winter morning	3	17	18
Winter evening	44	44	52

A check on the reliability of the individual sites is afforded by substituting the value of ϵ just found in each of the equations (4.5) and so finding the values of the temperatures, which are otherwise concealed in the solution. We are not here seeking to find temperatures in Megalithic times. The object in giving these values is to establish the credibility of the various sight lines. It will be seen that with the exception of the summer morning temperature the values are all within $20°$ of what we might expect. The low value of the summer morning temperature immediately casts doubt on Peninver as a solstitial site. We have already seen that the stone is not orientated on the foresight assumed. There seems to be only one way of reconciling this line and that is to raise the value of k to $1\cdot5$ or more. On the whole it seems better to ignore Peninver and instead to assume that the summer morning temperature was $40\,°F$. Doing this and again solving the equations gives the values shown in the last column of Table 4.2. The temperatures obtained seem to be reasonable and so we shall take $\epsilon = 23°\ 54'\cdot2$.

There are other possible sources of error apart from those already mentioned; e.g. the sites may belong to different dates or geological movements may have affected the altitudes of the foresights. The fact that all sites are in one district (south Argyllshire) suggests that all may belong to the same century. One would expect that serious geological movement would produce a scatter in the temperatures, but the discrepancy in the Peninver line would need over 50 feet of vertical movement to explain it. This is a most unlikely movement.

There is not a large enough number of sites to permit a standard error to be calculated, but we can make a guess and say that the result of this investigation is that

$$\epsilon = 23°\ 54'\cdot2 \pm 0'\cdot7,$$

which corresponds to a mean date of 1750 B.C.±100 years. Sufficient data have been given in the figures and tables to enable anyone to carry out their own analysis. It seems unlikely that any great improvement will be made until other sites have been found and all have been measured to an accuracy of $\pm20''$ under conditions approximating to those under which they were used, that is with clear skies at sundown or sunrise.

5

THE LUNAR OBSERVATORIES

5.1. FOR anyone who wishes to understand and appreciate how far our fore-fathers in these islands had advanced intellectually in the first half of the second millennium B.C., by far the most important sites are Temple Wood in Argyllshire and Mid Clyth in Caithness. Fortunately these are both relatively complete. The first shows unequivocally how lunar observations were made and the second demonstrates the method by which they were reduced. A modicum of mathematics is needed for an understanding of Mid Clyth, but Temple Wood can be understood by anyone who cares to follow the astronomical explanations in Chapter 2.

This chapter contains particulars of Temple Wood and other sites that may have been similarly equipped before they were despoiled. The Caithness sites are dealt with in Chapter 9.

5.2. Temple Wood, A 2/8, NR 827979

The little circle, with inner ring and kist, at Temple Wood lies on the west side of the narrow road at Netherlargie just south of Kilmartin. Across the road in the meadows stands the impressive line of menhirs shown in the survey in Fig. 5.1. The main line consists of five menhirs S_1, S_2, S_3, S_4, and S_5, varying in height from 7 to $9\frac{1}{2}$ feet. The largest S_1 has a number of cup marks cut on it and has four small upright slabs grouped round it. Some 10 yards along the line to the south-west there was, when the ground survey was made in 1939, a small group of small stones, marked Q, three upright and one fallen. The fallen slab is now missing. Temple Wood itself lies about 980 feet from S_1 at about 315°.

Looking from the menhirs *over the circle* there is seen a small but well-defined notch A (inset (*b*)) in the hill horizon about $1\frac{1}{4}$ miles distant. This notch formed the principal foresight for the Moon at its most northerly position during the major standstill. It will be appreciated that for work of the highest accuracy, provided a foresight is unambiguous, smallness is an advantage: the notch at Mid Clyth is still smaller, but again is unambiguous.

The ground at the menhirs is not perfectly flat and so separate determinations had to be made of the notch coordinates (azimuth and altitude) from Q, S_3, S_5, and S_6. During various visits over a dozen independent sun/

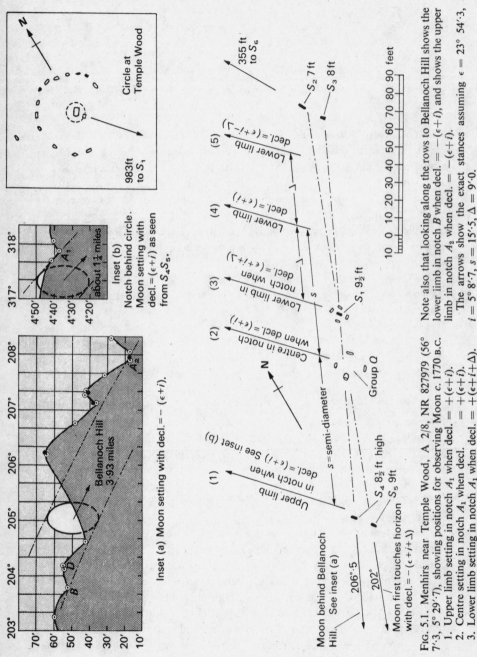

Inset (a) Moon setting with decl. = − (ε+i).

Inset (b)
Notch behind circle.
Moon setting with
decl. = (ε+i) as seen
from S_4S_5.

Circle at Temple Wood

983ft to S_1

355 ft to S_6

S_2 7 ft
S_3 8 ft

(5) Lower limb decl. = (ε+i−L)

(4) Lower limb decl. = (ε+i)

(3) Lower limb in notch when decl. = (ε+i+L)

(2) Centre in notch when decl. = (ε+i)

S_1 9½ ft

s = semi-diameter

Group Q

(1) Upper limb in notch when decl. = (ε+i) See inset (b)

S_4 8½ ft high
S_5 9ft

Moon behind Bellanoch Hill. See inset (a)

206°·5
202°

Moon first touches horizon with decl. = −(ε+i+Δ)

Bellanoch Hill 3·93 miles

about 1¼ miles

10 0 10 20 30 40 50 60 70 80 90 feet

Fig. 5.1. Menhirs near Temple Wood, A 2/8, NR 827979 (56° 7′·3, 5° 29′·7), showing positions for observing Moon c. 1770 B.C.
1. Upper limb setting in notch A_1 when decl. = +(ε+i).
2. Centre setting in notch A_1 when decl. = +(ε+i).
3. Lower limb setting in notch A_1 when decl. = +(ε+i+Δ).
4. Lower limb setting in notch A_1 when decl. = +(ε+i).

Note also that looking along the rows to Bellanoch Hill shows the lower iimb in notch B when decl. = −(ε+i), and shows the upper limb in notch A_2 when decl. = −(ε+i).
The arrows show the exact stances assuming ε = 23° 54′·3, i = 5° 8′·7, s = 15′·5, Δ = 9′·0.

theodolite observations were made in order to be quite certain of the particulars. The final results are given in the first part of Table 5.1.

For comparison with the observed values we may take the obliquity of the ecliptic $\epsilon = 23° 54'\cdot3$, $i = 5° 8'\cdot7$, the semidiameter $s = 15'\cdot5$, and the perturbation $\Delta = 9'$. With these we obtain the values in the last column. The agreement speaks for itself. The stones $S_5\,S_4$ form an alignment pointing to the notch and the group Q is orientated in the same direction, as are the faces

Table 5.1. *Measured declinations at Temple Wood*, A 2/8

Backsight	Foresight	Azimuth	Altitude	Declination observed	Expected declination		
Over circle							
$S_4\,S_5$	Notch A	317° 52'·5	4° 37'·2	+29° 19'·1	$\epsilon+i+s$	=	+29° 18'·5
Group Q	Notch A	317 12·6	4 37·7	29 2·5	$\epsilon+i$	=	29 3·0
S_1	Notch A	316 59·0	4 37·7	28 56·5	$\epsilon+i-s+\Delta$	=	28 56·5
$S_2\,S_3$	Notch A	316 1·6	4 38·7	28 32·6	See text		
S_6	Notch A	315 19	4 54	28 28	See text		
		Mean $(\epsilon+i) =$ 29° 3'·0					
To Bellanoch Hill							
$S_?$	Notch A_2	207° 56'	0° 18'	−28° 48'	$-(\epsilon+i-s) =$		−28° 47'·5
S_1	Notch B	203 46	0 52	−29 20	$-(\epsilon+i+s) =$		−29 18·5
		Mean = −29° 4'					

Assumed height of eye is 5·5 feet. The 'expected declinations' assume $\epsilon = 23° 54'\cdot3$, $i = 5° 8'\cdot7$, $s = 15'\cdot5$, $\Delta = 9'\cdot0$.

of the large menhir S_1. From these three positions we obtain the lunar declinations shown. The stones $S_2\,S_3$ do not indicate the notch, but form an alignment with S_6. Consequently we do not expect agreement and in fact do not find it. These stones must have provided information of a different kind, as we shall see later.

Perhaps the best method of demonstrating how accurately the stones are placed is to calculate the ideal stake positions for the various cases using the above values for ϵ, s, and Δ. In Fig. 5.1 these positions are shown by arrows. The arrows marked (1) and (4) show the stances for the upper and lower limbs when the declination is $\epsilon+i$. Almost midway between these is the stance for the Moon's centre, arrow (2). Arrows (3) and (5) show the mean upper and lower limits of the perturbation, i.e. the declinations $\epsilon+i-s+\Delta$ and $\epsilon+i-s-\Delta$. Was there a stone, now removed, at (5)?

But it is impossible to observe to the Moon's centre. What then was the reason for the group Q? The answer must be that the builders made use of the best possible observing technique, which is to have two observers, one concentrating on the upper limb and one on the lower. If the ground was reasonably level the point midway between their stake positions would then correspond to the Moon's centre and would be used with the group Q (see also Chapter 10). The advantage of this method is that it averages two people's work and incidentally also gets rid of the errors produced by the changes in the Moon's semidiameter.

It may be noticed that the distance between the two observers' stakes gives a measure of the Moon's apparent diameter, and so the changes in diameter produced by the changes in the Moon's distance would have shown up.

It is interesting to see that with the Moon in its extreme northerly position $(\epsilon+i+\Delta)$ the stance for the lower limb was at S_1, the largest menhir and that distinguished by having cup marks and by the group of stones round it. These small stones show roughly the limits of error produced by the variation in Δ, which is of the order of an arc minute. Is it fanciful to imagine that the stance for the Moon's centre is a group with no centre stone, reminding one that there is no mark at the centre of the disc to which observation could be made?

5.3. The line to the south-west

In one respect the lunar site at Temple Wood has something in common with the solstitial site at Ballochroy (A 4/4). In both the eye is directed across the line by the individual slabs pointing to the required foresight in the north-west, and in both the direction of the alignment itself shows the required foresight in the south-west. At Ballochroy the foresight is the fall of Cara to the west, and at Temple Wood it is the deep dip to the west of Bellanoch Hill, through which runs the road to Loch Sween (see Fig. 5.1, inset (a)).

At present at the menhirs Bellanoch Hill is hidden by intervening groups of trees. This made the accurate determination of the profile a somewhat complicated operation. By running a long accurate traverse round the woods a point P_1 was established 4835 feet from the stone S_1 at 210° 52' and 19 feet higher. From P_1 the azimuth and altitude of numerous points on the profile were measured. These were then reduced to what they would have been if viewed from S_1. They are shown on Fig. 5.1, inset (a) by open rings. Since the range of hills is not simply a two-dimensional silhouette, but has depth, ideally the point P_1 ought to be on the line from S_1 to the point being measured. In fact it had to be over 300 feet to the right. To check if any serious error was thereby being introduced, a second point P_2 was established 200 feet nearer the line, but from this position trees still further forward obscured the left end of the profile. The points found by using P_2 are shown by filled rings. It appears that the profile is established to about $\pm1'$. It is not possible to obtain greater accuracy until the trees have been removed, both from the line and from the slopes of Bellanoch Hill itself. The measurements were made in the spring before the leaves made matters completely impossible. An earlier cruder attempt gave for the main points almost identical values, and so it is believed that no serious error is present.

The importance of this profile becomes apparent when the last two lines of Table 5.1 are examined. It will be seen that the main dip at A_2 gave the upper limb when the Moon's declination was $-(\epsilon+i)$, while the first dip at B gave the lower limb position with the same declination. The point where the Moon in its extreme southerly position first touched the horizon is given by the line $S_2\,S_1\,S_5$.

When Dr. William MacGregor and I first surveyed the Temple Wood site in 1939 we recorded what seemed to be the remains of a cairn 265 feet from S_1 at an azimuth of 302°. The ploughing in 1969 showed that a hard, slightly raised area was still visible. This may be the remains of a large burial cairn similar to the others in the linear cemetery that runs through the site, but it hardly seems large enough. A much more intriguing explanation will be suggested in the next paragraph.

5.4. Temple Wood and the alignments lie on a stretch of level land in the valley, surrounded by hills of varying height. On this plane the builders found a position from which Bellanoch Hill and the notch behind the circle gave the required declinations, positive *and* negative. Behind the circle the ground rises, but there was just room to place the circle 980 feet from the stone S_1, and, as we shall see in Chapter 9, this was the extrapolation length ($4G$) for the Bellanoch foresight. The extrapolation length for the notch is 272 feet and this is roughly the distance (265 feet) to the hard patch of ground mentioned in the last paragraph. There is thus the possibility that the Temple Wood circle and a similar structure on the hard patch contained the apices of the extrapolation triangles. Does this provide an explanation of the little stone box on the inner ring at Temple Wood?

But, after finding a site satisfying the conditions, there remained the extremely difficult task of establishing the stones to give the *mean* stances at the standstills with the kind of accuracy that has been demonstrated to exist. Without some extrapolation method the task could well have taken many decades and even when the positions were established the whole observatory would have been impossible to operate. Granted that an extrapolation scheme was in use there were still difficulties. It is true that the relatively high altitudes, especially of the notch, got rid of refraction troubles, but there remained the difficulties produced by the varying distance of the Moon as it described its elliptical orbit round the Earth. This causes parallax and semidiameter to vary by some 6 per cent on each side of the mean values. Thus parallax may sometimes be as high as 61·5 arc minutes and sometimes as low as 53·9. It is true that at Temple Wood the effect of parallax on declination is some 10 per cent less, but how did the erectors deal with anomalies of this kind? It is becoming clear that they worked at a site until they had established backsights for the *mean* positions. Temple Wood is one of the best examples for showing this because it has foresights for both $(\epsilon+i)$ and $-(\epsilon+i)$. The declinations given in Table 5.1 entitled 'observed' have been calculated from the measured azimuths and altitudes using the refraction in Table 3.1 and the mean parallax, namely 57'·0. It will be seen that the same value of $\epsilon+i$ suits both foresights to within a minute or so. Had we used a parallax of, say, 60' the positive values of the declinations would have risen by nearly 2'·8 and the negative value from Bellanoch Hill would have risen algebraically, i.e. fallen numerically, by the same amount. Another way of putting it is to say that we can at Temple Wood determine the value of the parallax that best fits the profiles, and it turns out to be close to the mean value 57'. We shall see in § 7.5 that we must expect to find mean parallax at any site, so that this only tells us that our measurements are correct and that both foresights were used together.

It will be seen that this site gives us so much information that it must be regarded as one of the most important, if not the most important, of the sites in Britain. A careful study of the stones shows, without reference to any other site, that the Megalithic builders were capable of erecting real lunar observatories. It remains for Mid Clyth to show how the necessary extrapolation was probably done.

5.5. For any serious worker making a detailed study of Temple Wood some further points may be raised. The group Q lies a foot or two low relative to the general line of the row. Consequently, if it was obtained by bisecting on the ground the distance between stakes placed for the upper and lower limbs, the value of the declination we have obtained by measurements to the notch made at Q will show a declination about an arc minute too high. Taking this into consideration and giving rather more weight to the Q value, it seems that the present investigation shows a mean value for $\epsilon+i$ of about 29° 2'·5 with an uncertainty of less than 1'. This corresponds (with $i = 5° 8' 43''$) to a date of 1700 B.C.$\pm$100 years. If it is ever possible to obtain a directly measured profile of Bellanoch Hill it might be possible to improve on this estimate. But the theory developed in § 7.5 shows that it is not safe to use this for dating unless we know that the work of erection was spread over at least a century.

The serious student of the site should also consider the possible uses of the alignment $S_3 S_2 S_6$. With the measured hill horizon altitudes it does not in either direction give any of the usual stellar, lunar, or solar declinations (see Thom 1967, table 8.1). We propose to examine the line as providing advance information about what was to be expected at the coming standstill. On the date of the standstill (taken as the date of the maximum of the 18·6-year cycle) would the perturbation wobble be at a maximum, at a minimum, or at some intermediate stage? The two extreme cases are illustrated diagrammatically in Fig. 5.2 (a) and (b). These show, as in Fig. 2.3, the perturbation superimposed on the long-period oscillation. In Fig. 5.2 (a) we see the maxima occurring simultaneously. Then, 260 days earlier (i.e. $1\frac{1}{2} \times 173$ days), there is a minimum showing a declination of the lower limb of 28° 29'. This is very close to the declination actually observed from the stone S_6, namely 28° 28'.

In Fig. 5.2 (b) we see that when a minimum of the perturbation occurs *at* the standstill, the previous minimum shows a lower limb declination of 28° 34', and from Table 5.1, this is close to the declination of the notch measured

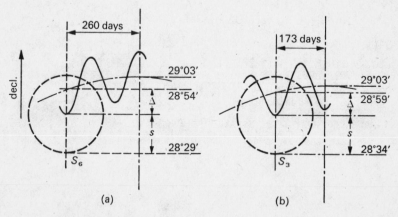

(a)   (b)

FIG. 5.2. Use of the line $S_3 S_2 S_6$ to give advance information regarding the conditions to be expected at the coming standstill. (a) Declination observed at $S_6 = 28° 28'$. (b) Declination observed at $S_3 = 28° 33'$.

from stone S_3. The minimum might of course happen anywhere between S_3 and S_6, but the position found would always be a guide. Starting to observe about 300 days early and operating on the line $S_3 S_6$ (produced if necessary), the extrapolated stake positions could be established for every lunation. These positions would oscillate with the perturbation, but if the extreme right position (minimum declination) came at S_6 then the observer expected that conditions were as in Fig. 5.2 (a). If it came at S_3 conditions were as in Fig. 5.2 (b). For reasons given in § 7.5, however, this method of predicting the conditions could not have been accurate on all occasions.

The date of a node can be more accurately obtained by observation than that of a maximum. It follows that at a highly developed observatory like Temple Wood the workers would, for eclipse prediction, almost certainly prefer to use the nodes of the perturbation oscillation. This view is supported by finding that the group Q shows exactly $\epsilon + i$, which is the node, provided it occurred at or near the standstill. By making observations as described above on the line $S_3 S_6$, the observers may have hoped to determine in advance which nodes were most suitable, i.e. which nodes occurred nearest to the standstill.

5.6. Ballymeanach or Duncracaig, A 2/12, NR 833964

This site lies 1 mile from Temple Wood in a south-west direction; in fact the two sites are almost intervisible. Here we find:

(1) An impressive alignment of four slabs, 13, 12, 9, and 9 feet high,
(2) An alignment of two large slabs, 8 and 10 feet high,
(3) A fallen hole stone,
(4) A circle or cairn,
(5) A loose stone between (1) and (4).

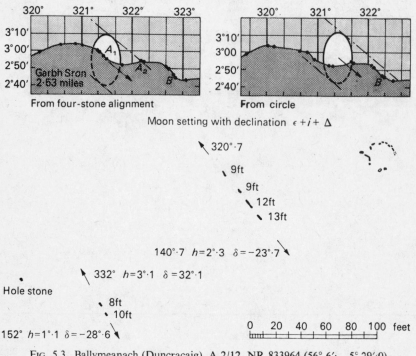

FIG. 5.3. Ballymeanach (Duncracaig), A 2/12, NR 833964 (56° 6′· , 5ᶜ 29′·0).

These lie some 1300 feet from Duncracaig Cairn and there are remains of several other cairns around the site, some now hidden in the wood. The small-scale plan in Fig. 5.3 has been reduced from a survey made in 1939.

The size of the stones in the four-stone alignment shows that it was important. It served at least two purposes. To the south-east it gives the declination of the Sun at the winter solstice, but trees now prevent any possible foresight from being seen. To the north-west it indicates the top of the hill Garbh Sron. In the inset we see the Moon setting in its extreme northerly position, i.e. with declination $\epsilon+i+\Delta$. The centre is marked by the declivity at A_1 parallel to the direction of movement, and the upper limb by a rock A_2.

This rock is just large enough to be visible without optical aid and so provided a very accurate foresight. To ensure accuracy in the coordinates of these points several visits were made with independent determinations on each occasion. The particulars are given in Table 5.2, which also contains other information of use in interpolating to other positions. For example, at a point midway between the alignment and the circle the declination of B is 29° 28′·5, which is about $(\epsilon+i+s+\Delta)$, and there is a stone lying in this position.

Table 5.2. *Declinations measured at Ballymeanach*, A 2/12

Backsight	Foresight	Azimuth	Altitude	Declination		
4 stones	A_1	321° 30′	2° 56′	29° 13′·6	$\epsilon+i+\Delta$	$= 29° 12′$
	B	322 51	2 45	29 34		
	A_2	322 13	2 54	29 28 ·5	$\epsilon+i+\Delta+s = 29° 27′·5$	
'Circle'	A_1	320 53	2 57	29 0		
	B	322 18	2 46	29 23		
	A_2	321 40	2 55	29 16		

The two-stone alignment seems to indicate the Moon rising in its most southerly position. Trees obscure the view, making it impossible to see if there is a foresight on the line. Other possible lines are suggested in Thom 1967. The value of $\epsilon+i$ found at Temple Wood applies to the Ballymeanach site within about a minute.

It seems likely that here, as at Temple Wood, there were other stones, now removed, that would show the other cases. Enough data have been given to enable suspected positions of these missing stones to be checked. For example, the two-stone alignment could never have been lunar with the foresights A_1, B, or A_2. Any other backsights for these foresights must have been on the right of the four-stone alignment.

5.7. Fowlis Wester, P 1/10, NN 924250

Just to the north of Fowlis Wester near Crief there is an interesting lunar observatory. Here we find two ellipses, each with properties associated with Megalithic ellipses. The line joining their centres gives in both directions the small positive declinations that we expect on theoretical grounds to find for the equinoctial Sun rising and setting. The east ellipse has stones round it suggesting an outer ring and indeed the *Statistical Account* mentions 'concentric circles'.

If one stands at the centre of the east ellipse E, and looks along the major axis, one sees how the menhir M hides all the hill Creag na Criche (inset centre of Fig. 5.4) except the point A (inset left). This point A has exactly the declination of the upper limb of the Moon rising at the standstill, i.e

($\epsilon+i+s$). From the large boulder N the declination of the same point is ($\epsilon+i+s+\Delta$).

The setting position of the Moon is indicated by the axis of the more ruinous ellipse W to the west. No foresight now appears on the horizon, but as it is only slightly over a mile distant a small artificial mark would have

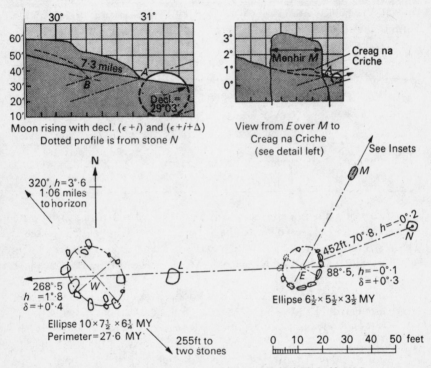

Moon rising with decl. ($\epsilon+i$) and ($\epsilon+i+\Delta$)
Dotted profile is from stone N

View from E over M to
Creag na Criche
(see detail left)

FIG. 5.4. Fowlis Wester, P 1/10, NN 924250 (56° 24'·3, 3° 44'·6).

been sufficient. The ground on the hilltop ridge has not yet been examined to see if any trace remains. Let us *assume* that the foresight was on the low flat apex at azimuth 320°·2, $h = 3°$ 34' as seen from W. We then find the declinations shown in Table 5.3.

Table 5.3. *Declinations of assumed foresight from four points*

Backsight	Declination	'Expected' declination	
W	29° 3'	$\epsilon+i$	= 29° 3'
L	28 57	$\epsilon+i-s+\Delta$	= 28 56
E	28 47	$\epsilon+i-s$	= 28 47
M	28 37	$\epsilon+i-s-\Delta$	= 28 38

The agreement with the values in the last column is sufficiently close to make it seem likely that there was a foresight in the assumed position. The west ellipse would then have served the same purpose as group Q at Temple Wood in that it showed the Moon's centre at the node of the perturbation

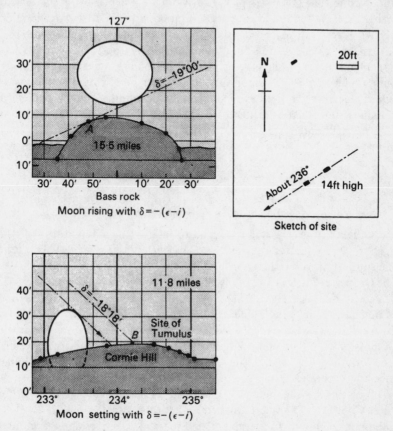

FIG. 5.5. Standing Stones of Lundin, P 4/1, NO 40475 02710 (56° 12′ 48″, 2° 57′ 36″).

oscillation ($\Delta = 0$). The east ellipse, as we have seen, definitely showed $\Delta = 0$ for the upper limb on foresight A, and probably showed $\Delta = 0$ for the lower limb on the assumed foresight in the north-west.

No explanation has yet been found for the two stones and other indefinite traces on the south side of the site. The distance of these stones from the east ellipse is about 210 feet and this *may* relate to the extrapolation length $4G$ (200 feet) for the setting foresight. Some other lengths on the site are compared with G in Table 9.1, but the agreements are probably accidental. They are given to support the idea that the size of a site is often related to G or $4G$.

5.9. Lundin Links, P 4/1, NO 405027

This impressive site now consists of two 14-foot menhirs and a smaller one about 100 feet to the north. It was obviously an important site, so placed on flat ground that there was plenty of room for geometrical extrapolation. The alignment is seen to indicate the setting point of the Moon at the minor standstill. Trees and houses now block the view, but as the new large-scale O.S. maps are now available for this district it was possible to construct a reasonably accurate profile of Cormie Hill. In good seeing conditions a large tumulus could have been seen on the Moon's disc, and the tumulus shown on the Ordnance Survey happens to indicate the upper limb when the declination was about $-(\epsilon-i-\Delta)$. When the Moon set on Cormie Hill it would rise on the Bass Rock, and we see how the stones were so placed that the lower limb just grazed the Rock when the declination was $-(\epsilon-i)$. Houses now block the view, but a profile was measured from the high ground behind and then corrected to what it would be from the stones.

5.9. Crois Mhic-Aoida, Beinn an Tuirc, Kintyre, A 4/9, NR 734351

This is difficult of access, but has much of interest, including a row of what are perhaps earth houses surrounded by a ring of large stones. This last lies to the south of the area shown in Fig. 5.6.

The Ordnance Survey shows only one stone. It is true that there is now only one vertical, but a second is still standing, although leaning over. The moor does not have many stray boulders, but around and near these two menhirs there are about two dozen large stones or boulders. The site is covered with peat, moss, etc., so there may be many more that I did not find. We have here all the signs that this was a most important site. It is undoubtedly lunar. Notice how accurately the fall of Beinn Bheigeir 23 miles away in Islay shows the Moon setting at the minor standstill with declination $(\epsilon-i-\Delta)$, and how the hill Cnoc Moy 14 miles to the south deals with the major standstill. Standing on the impressive large flat slab marked S one sees how accurately the main standing stone M is orientated on the southern setting point. There is now little to indicate Beinn Bheigeir unless one accepts the general run of stones seen in the survey. The hard patch with stones round it may be of interest.

It has not yet been possible to get an accurate theodolite up to the site, so the check points added to the profiles constructed from the Ordnance Survey may be a minute or two in error, having been obtained by time/azimuth observations with a light instrument.

The extensive nature of the site will make the task of prodding for other stones somewhat laborious. But this ought to be undertaken soon lest draining and planting moves the stones. One ought also to look for signs of a backsight further to the north-west from which the declination $-(\epsilon+i)$

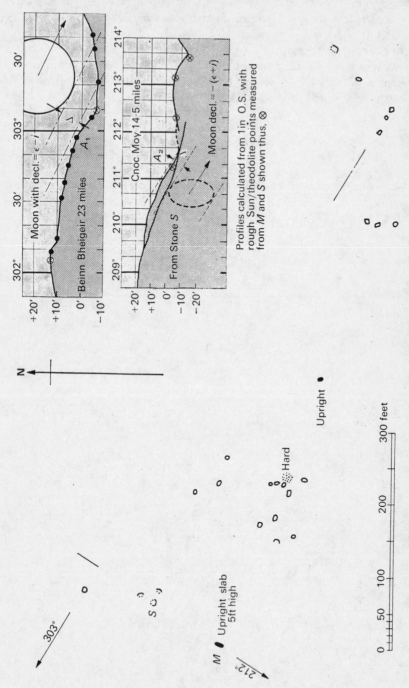

Fig. 5.6. Crois Mhic-Aoida, Beinn an Tuirc, A 4/9, NR 73443509 (55° 33'·0, 5° 35'·4). About 950 ft O.D.

would be indicated in addition to $-(\epsilon+i-\Delta)$. Anyone going there, however, must be prepared for a steep scramble and walk from the end of the forestry road in Glen Ifferdale.

The extrapolation length G is about 560 feet for the Beinn Bheigeir line and 820 feet for Cnoc Moy. There is room for either of these to be recorded among the stones shown. These values have been calculated for level ground, although the ground cannot be said to be level over all.

6

OBSERVING SITES

6.1. IN addition to the fully equipped observatories like Temple Wood, we find many places where an alignment, or a single stone, marks the stance for seeing the Moon graze a distant foresight at the standstill. Some of these sites may be the last remnant of a former observatory, but some are so placed that freedom of movement on the level was so restricted that it is difficult to see how the station did any more than show that on a certain date the Moon happened to be in one of the limiting positions when it rose or set on the foresight. It will be understood how limited was the use of such a site compared with a site where extrapolation was possible.

Particulars regarding such of these sites as are known will now be given.

6.2. Escart, Kintyre, A 4/1, NR 846667

This impressive alignment of five menhirs stands at the farm of Escart on the south shore of West Loch Tarbert. The farmer, Mr. Mitchell, suggests that the two stones at each end of the line point to the setting position of the midwinter Sun, but the particulars have not yet been determined. A wall now divides the alignment in two, preventing direct verification that there is a clear sight line through the menhirs, but the careful survey of the bases of the stones shows that this is probable. Because of the trees that block the view, the profile of Sheirdrim Hill shown in Fig. 6.1 had to be measured from a point a short distance along the line and referred to the stones by calculation, but it is believed to be within a minute or two of the truth.

Here again we have a site for both a lunar and a solar line. The difficulty of trying to satisfy both is enhanced by the peculiarly restricted area of level ground available. These difficulties may have forced the decision to make the line indicate $-(\epsilon+i-\Delta)$ instead of $-(\epsilon+i+\Delta)$.

6.3. High Park, Kintyre, A 4/2, NR 695258

The large menhir here is close to the lonely farm of High Park some miles north of Campbelltown. The measured profile shown contains foresights for $-(\epsilon+i)$ and $-(\epsilon+i+\Delta)$ with the rising Moon.

The setting Moon with the same declinations grazed the shoulder of the nearby hill, but this hill is so close that it could only have acted as a warning.

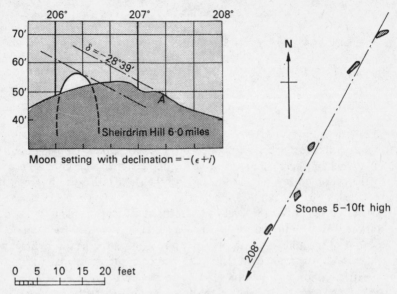

Moon setting with declination $=-(\epsilon+i)$

0   5   10   15   20   feet

FIG. 6.1. Alignment at Escart, A 4/1, NR '846667 (55° 50′ 46″, 5° 26′ 26″).

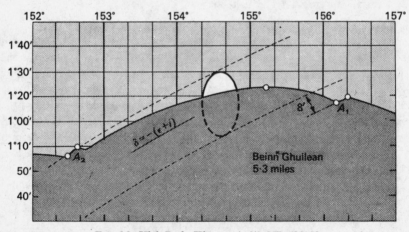

FIG. 6.2. High Park, Kintyre, A 4/2, NR 695258.

6.4. Beacharr, Kintyre, A 4/5, NR 692433

Here on a prominent ridge overlooking the coast stands one of the tallest menhirs in Scotland. Near the stone are the remains of the 'long cairn' well known to archaeologists. The measured profile in Fig. 6.3 shows that the sharp dip between Beinn an Oir and Beinn Shiantaidh provides a lunar declination of about $\epsilon+i-\Delta$. Behind Beacharr farm, which lies in a hollow behind the ridge, there is a level raised stretch before the hillside again rises steeply. The observer's position may have been on this plateau with the menhir silhouetted on the Paps. Only excavation can decide if the slight irregularities in the ground are artificial, natural, or modern. But the size of the stone indicates a lunar site to which considerable importance was attached by the erectors.

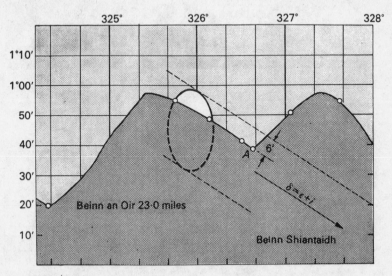

FIG. 6.3. Beacharr, Kintyre, A 4/5, NR 692433 (55° 37'·7, 5° 40'·0).

6.5. Campbelltown, Kintyre, A 4/14, NR 72372125

Above the town on the north side of the loch there is an impressive menhir about 11 feet high. The profile of the hills across the loch is shown in Fig. 6.4. It will be seen that there are three foresights for the Moon as it crossed the meridian. This profile can now be accepted as correct to ±1′ and has the advantage of being so high as to be free from refraction anomalies. At no other site do we find foresights for the Moon so near the meridian.

6.6. Carrach an Tarbert, Gigha, A 4/17, NR 655523

As the name implies, this large 8-foot-high menhir stands on the isthmus near the north end of Gigha, which lies off the west coast of Kintyre. This position makes it possible to see to the north-west and to the north-east, and in Fig. 6.5 interesting profiles are shown in both directions. It seems almost certain that the stone is placed so that when the Moon was in its extreme northerly position the upper limb rose on the summit of Meall Reamhar in Knapdale, as shown in the lower figure. On the same evening the Moon would set over the Paps of Jura as shown in the upper figure, but until a

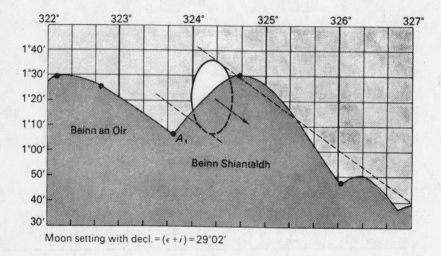

Fig. 6.4. Campbelltown, A 4/14, NR 72372125 (55° 25'·9, 5° 35'·9). Profile across loch from large menhir.

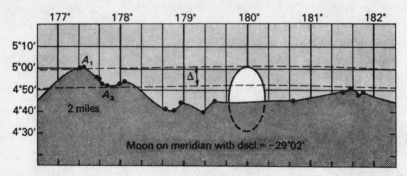

Moon setting with decl. = $(\epsilon + i) = 29°02'$

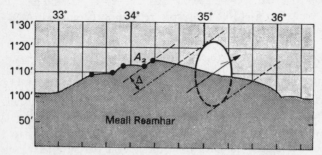

Moon rising with decl = $\epsilon + i = 29°02'$

Fig. 6.5. Carrach an Tarbert, Gigha, A 4/17, NR 655523 (55° 42'·4, 5° 43'·9). Two profiles from the 8-ft menhir. Measured points shown are to ±1'.

more detailed profile is available it is not possible to say that this was used. The ground is so restricted that it must have been difficult to arrange both sight lines from one stone.

6.7. Knockstaple, Kintyre, A 4/19, NR 703125

This large slab stands on the high ground behind Knockstaple Beg. It is visible from the Campbelltown road but not from the farm. It stands about 11 feet high, and as it is over 5 feet wide with flat faces the indicated azimuth 326° is reliable. From the stone the horizon profile is as shown in Fig. 6.6.

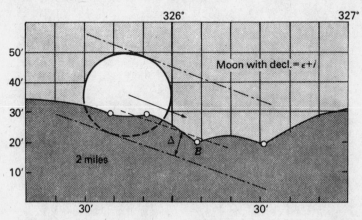

FIG. 6.6. Knockstaple, A 4/19, NR 703125 (55° 21'·1, 5° 37'·5). Profile from the stone, 11 feet high×6×1½ feet, orientated 326°.

It appears that the intended declination was $\epsilon+i+\Delta$. There is plenty of room round the stone and there are one or two small stones lying nearby.

6.8. Kilberry, Knapdale, A 3/5, NR 707670

This 5-foot stone is wedged in the rock on a promontory, and is roughly orientated on the foresight in Fig. 6.7. It shows the Sun setting with declination $+0°·6$, which is within a few arc minutes of the expected declination ($+0°·44$) at the Megalithic equinox (Thom 1967).

6.9. Dunadd, A 2/13, NR 840933

Across the farm road from Dunadd Hill, in the field beside the River Add, lies a large slab about 13 feet by 5 feet. This was standing in living memory, but is said to have fallen during a gale. Its orientation before it fell might have been north-west. Between the farm and the bridge there is a small upright stone bearing about 328° from the fallen menhir. This is some 3° too great to be lunar, but it suggested examining the horizon near this azimuth. The result of careful measurement is shown in Fig. 6.8. The declination of the point *A* with lunar parallax is 29° 18'. Deducting the semidiameter leaves 29° 2½', or $\epsilon + i$ in 1700 B.C. The large size of the menhir supports the idea that we have here the remains of a lunar site. There may well have been many more stones, now built into the farm, or indeed into the bridge.

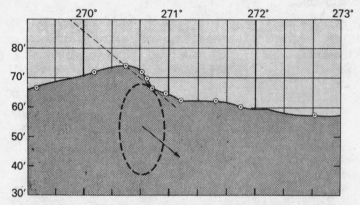

FIG. 6.7. Kilberry, Knapdale, A 3/5, NR 707670 (55° 50'·4, 5° 39'·7). Sun setting on Dubh Bheinn with decl. = +0° 36' as seen from the stone, which is roughly orientated on the foresight.

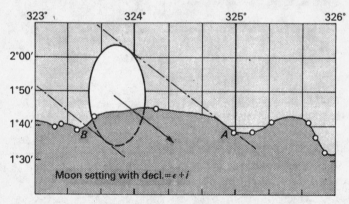

FIG. 6.8. Dunadd, A 2/13, NR 840933 (56° 5'·1, 5° 28'·3).

6.10. Camus an Stacca, Jura, A 6/1, NR 455647

The 12-foot high, wide slab here has an azimuth of 154°. No foresight was seen, but the declination is close to that of the Moon rising at the major standstill. It would then set as shown in Fig. 6.9. This is a Sun/theodolite measured profile considered to be accurate. From the same stone the mountain, Sgorr nam Faoileann, across the Sound of Islay at 213° 40', has an altitude of 4° 9'·5 giving a declination of −24° 10'. This is the lower limb of the Sun at the winter solstice *c.* 1700 B.C., so that this may well be another solstitial site. In Chapter 10 we shall see how a site set up by observing the solstitial Sun could be used for predicting the date of the lunar standstill. The accuracy provided by Sgorr nam Faoileann is ample for this purpose, so here, as at Kintraw, one site served two purposes.

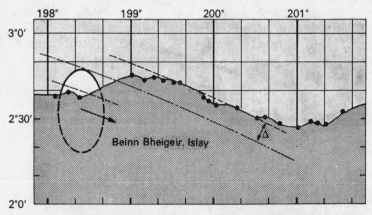

FIG. 6.9. Camus an Stacca, Jura, A 6/1, NR 455647 (55° 48′ 32″, 6° 2′ 50″). Moon setting over Beinn Bheigeir with decl. $= -(\epsilon+i)$ from the 12-foot stone. The mountain profile is considered to be accurate to $\pm 1'$.

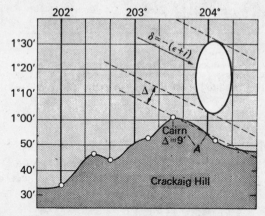

FIG. 6.10. Knockrome, Jura, A 6/4, NR 548715 (55° 52′ 27″, 5° 55′ 0″). From centre stone, orientated 200°.

6.11. Knockrome, Jura, A 6/4, NR 548715

Near the head of the bay opposite the north end of the Small Isles there is a line of three widely separated standing stones. The orientation of the centre stone draws attention to Crackaig Hill at the other end of the bay. The profile shown was measured by Sun/theodolite technique. The shoulder of the hill shows the extreme south position of the Moon's lower limb (Fig. 6.10).

6.12. Stillaig, A 10/5, NR 935678

Here there are two large menhirs about 2200 feet apart. The orientation of the south stone invites one to look to the north stone, which then appears as shown in Fig. 6.11. A recently measured profile of Cruach Breacain shows how it appears behind the stone. The profile may be inaccurate by a minute, but the line is definitely lunar. The extrapolation length is about 2800 feet, again of the same order as the length of the alignment. There is another small stone near the north stone, and there appear to be other remains near the line.

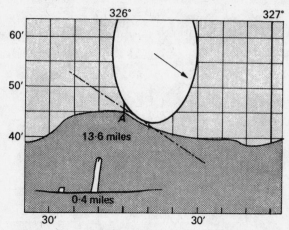

FIG. 6.11. Stillaig, A 10/5, NR 935678 (55° 51'·5, 5° 18'·0). View from south stone over north stone to Cruach Breacain and to the Moon setting with declination $\epsilon + i + \Delta$.

6.13. Muasdale, A 4/6, NP 678391

Near South Muasdale there is a large menhir that seems to use the same foresight (Beinn Bheigeir) as the Beinn an Tuirc stones (A 4/9), again for the minor standstill. As it has not been possible to obtain an accurately measured profile no data for the site will be given.

6.14. Quinish, Mull, M 1/3, NM 41365524

This site stands on the east side of the entrance to Loch Cuan in the north of Mull. Only one 10-foot-high menhir is now upright. The view to the north is obstructed by high ground, but the highest hill visible to the south, Carn Mhor, is indicated by the alignment. The profile as measured by a small theodolite is shown to contain foresights for upper and lower limb at the standstill. The extreme lowest position of the lower limb is given as at Knockrome by the hilltop (Fig. 6.12).

6.15. Dervaig, Mull, M 1/5, NM 440520

This long alignment was probably intended to show the Moon at the major standstill with declination $(\epsilon+i)$, setting on the west end of Canna, but verification of the foresight has not yet been possible. A plan will be found in Thom 1965, fig. 7.

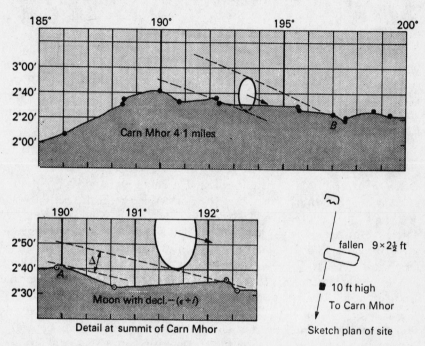

Detail at summit of Carn Mhor

Sketch plan of site

FIG. 6.12. Quinish, Mull, M 1/3, NM 41365524 (56° 37′ 4″, 6° 13′ 4″).

6.16. Bunessan, M 2/8, NM 398223

About a mile east from Bunessan in Mull there is a 6-foot menhir with the long sides orientated on a boulder on the near horizon. The azimuth 330°·7 and the altitude 0°·2 give a lunar declination of 29°·5, close to the upper limb in the extreme north position. No weight can be attached to this until the particulars have been verified.

6.17. Balemartin, Tiree, M 4/2, NM 974426

Near Balemartin in the island of Tiree there is a menhir about 12 feet high surrounded by what was perhaps a ring of stones. Some 60 yards to the north there is a second ring, which may have been set out as an ellipse 6½ by 6 MY. The distance between the foci would be exactly 2½ and the perimeter 19·64, so the usual Megalithic conditions for an ellipse would have been fulfilled.

The stone is irregular, but its flat faces might be said to indicate the hill Carnan Mhor, the peak of which is at 190° 12′ with an altitude of about 2° 48′. This gives a declination of −29° 27′, which is exactly −(ϵ+i+s+Δ). So here, as at Fowlis Wester, we have at a lunar site an ellipse behind a menhir. At Fowlis Wester the foresight is far enough away to make it unimportant whether the observer stands in the ellipse or at the menhir, but in Tiree the hill is so near that the observer's position is important. The site needs to be carefully surveyed before it is fully accepted.

Some distance to the west a stone (M 4/3) has one of its faces orientated on Carnan Mhor, showing a declination of about −23°·8, and at the other end of the island there seems to be a line for the summer solstice. If this is verified then there are lines for +ϵ and −ϵ of sufficient accuracy to enable the date of the standstill to be predicted by the method described in Chapter 10.

6.18. Callanish I, H 1/1, NB 213330

Details of this important site will be found in Thom 1965 and 1967. An accurate survey has been published twice by Somerville (1912). It needs a small correction in orientation, and Somerville seems to give horizon altitudes corrected for refraction. A good survey, but without horizon altitudes, was given by James (1867). Some undocumented re-erection of fallen stones (see Thom 1965, p. 150 and Thom 1967, p. 124), which took place in the nineteenth century, may have affected by a few minutes the azimuth of the main 'avenue'. The sides of this avenue as it now stands are at azimuths of 190°·6 (west side) and 189°·2 (east side). The profile of the horizon at this azimuth as calculated from the Ordnance Survey is shown in Fig. 6.13. It will be seen that we have here the Moon setting in its southerly position at the major standstill with the perturbation limits well shown. The distance to the foresight and the flat descent path of the Moon make G (see Chapter 8) so large that it is difficult to see where there was room for any extrapolation to be done. The site is, however, intervisible with Callanish V, and the information as to when the Moon *rose* in its limiting positions would have come from there, allowing the backsight at Callanish I to be established when the Moon *set* a few hours later.

6.19. Callanish V, H 1/5, NB 234299

The profile in Fig. 6.14 was carefully constructed from the old 6-in Ordnance Survey, which in this district is contoured at 25-foot intervals. It will be seen that here the erectors succeeded in finding a position from which the mountain profile shows the perturbation limits for the upper limb and one of the limits for the lower. Perhaps Ben Mhor was considered to give the mean, i.e. −(ϵ+i), with the lower limb. The ground round the site is not particularly

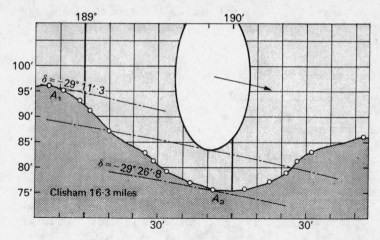

FIG. 6.13. Callanish I, H 1/1, NB 213330 (58° 11′·8, 6° 44′·6). View along the avenue to the south with Moon setting with declination $-(\epsilon + i)$.

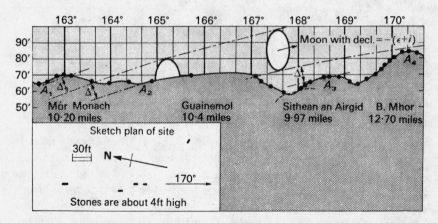

FIG. 6.14. View south from Callanish V, Tursachan Airidh nam Bidearan, H 1/5, NB 234299 (58° 10′ 13″·0, 6° 42′ 16″·3). Moon rising at major standstill with declination $-(\epsilon + i)$.

level, but this need not have prevented extrapolation from being carried out. One notes that the distance to the circle Callanish VII is almost exactly equal to G (1200 feet), and that the distance to the sites to the east is $4G$. More work needs to be done before any definite decision can be made as to how the site was operated. In Thom 1967 (fig. 11.4) I have suggested that there may be another lunar line from Callanish V to the north, and this was verified in 1972.

The whole group of circles and stones at the head of Loch Roag in the Callanish district needs to be thoroughly explored and accurately surveyed before we can learn all it has to teach us.

6.20. Leacach an Tigh Chloiche, H 3/11, NF 800669

This site is described in Thom 1967. A profile recalculated from the 1-in Ordnance Survey is given in Fig. 6.15, but it may be in error by several minutes. The perturbation limits are certainly rather larger than usual.

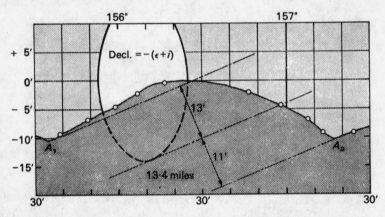

FIG. 6.15. Wiay from Leacach an Tigh Chloiche, H 3/11, NF 800669 (57° 34′ 38″, 7° 21′ 18″).

6.21. Corogle Burn, Glen Prosen, P 3/1, NO 349601

On a level stretch of ground on the left bank of the Burn of Corogle there is an alignment of four stones. It shows to the south a lunar declination of $-28°·9$, the upper limb when the declination is $-(\epsilon+i+\Delta)$, but since no foresight was noticed the accuracy depends on what can be determined from the alignment itself. Since the horizon is not far away it could have carried an artificial foresight. The extrapolation length is not much longer than the present length of the alignment, and since there are other stones outside the row there may have been other backsights or some extrapolation arrangement.

6.22. Kell Burn, G 9/13, NT 643642

This alignment of small stones is not on the Ordnance Survey. It lies just west of the road. It is about 310 feet long and so of itself gives a fairly accurate azimuth of 129° 50′. No foresight was noticed, but the declination indicated $(-19°·0)$ shows it to be a lunar site. The distance to the horizon is not known but may be about $2\frac{1}{2}$ miles, which makes $4G$ about 270 feet, of the same order as the length of the alignment. A plan will be found in Thom 1965 (fig. 10).

6.23. Haggstone Moor, Wigtownshire, G 3/2, NX 0772

The stone that gives the name to the moor may perhaps be the fallen menhir at 065726. But there are at least three other stones on the moor. Long Tom is nearly 6 feet high, and the Taxing Stone about 5 feet. The other stone, marked S on the key plan, is smaller.

Standing at Long Tom one sees about a mile away a mound or cairn, and behind this, 37 miles away, the Mull of Kintyre appears as shown in the first profile. The foresight was formed by 'The Gap' through which runs the road to the Mull lighthouse. This gives exactly $\epsilon-i+\Delta$ for the Moon's upper limb. Profiles are also given from the stone S and from the fallen menhir. It is almost certain that these sites make use of the two steps shown to give $\epsilon-i$, $\epsilon-i+\Delta$, and $\epsilon-i-\Delta$. The calculated value of the extrapolation length $4G$ at 3600 feet is of the same order as the distance across the whole site, so one ought to keep a look-out for other remains.

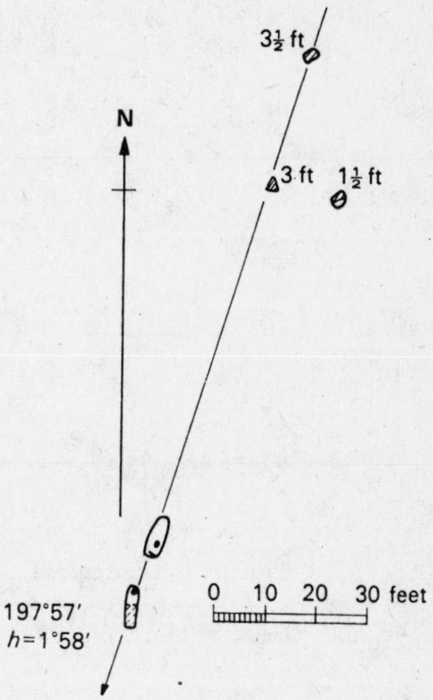

6.24. Clachan Direach, P 1/18, NN 925558

A plan of these stones will be found in Thom 1967 (fig. 12.14). Unfortunately

FIG. 6.16. Corogle Burn, Glen Prosen, P 3/1, NO 349601 (56° 43'·7, 3° 3'·8).

attempts to measure the profile were unsuccessful. The rapidly growing forest makes it now impossible. The accuracy of the constructed profile is so low that it cannot be used here. It is suggested that the name of these stones was perhaps Clachan Direach, the straight stones, rather than Clachan Diridh, but see Mitchell (1923).

6.25. Blakeley Moss, L 1/16, NY 06001402

Close to the east side of the road south from Ennerdale Bridge in Cumberland there is a good stone circle exactly 20 MY yards in diameter. Looking across the centre of the circle from the highest stone one sees the escarpment of Screel Hill in Dumfriesshire. We find elsewhere that one of the stones in a circle is diametrically opposite the outlier. If there ever were an outlier showing Screel Hill, the ground is such that it would have been removed when the road was built. The indication may be weak, but it is interesting to see how

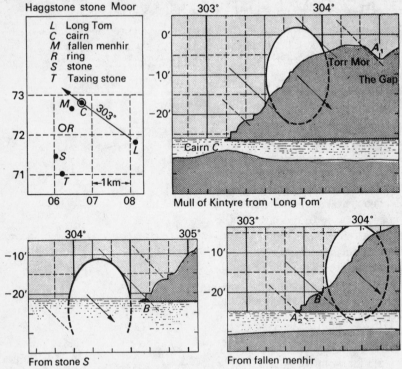

FIG. 6.17. Haggstone Moor, Wigtonshire, G 3/2, NX 0772. Long Tom is at 08167182 (55° 0′·2, 5° 0′·0). On each profile the Moon is shown setting with decl. $= (\epsilon - i)$.

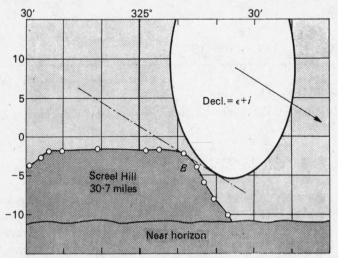

FIG. 6.18. Blakeley Moss, L 1/16, NY 06001402 (54° 30′ 46″, 3° 27′ 11″). Moon at mean max. declination.

exactly the shoulder of the hill gave the lower limb when the declination was ($\epsilon+i$). (Fig. 6.18).

6.26. Parc-y-Meirw, W 9/7, SM 999359

This alignment of four large menhirs lies 3 or 4 miles from Fishguard and is undoubtedly lunar. Because of rising ground it cannot have been intended for use to the south-east. The azimuth of 301°·4 was first published (Thom

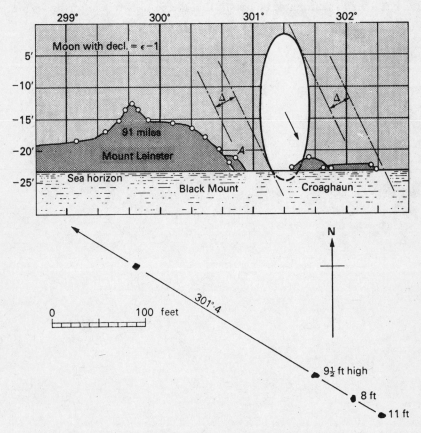

FIG. 6.19. Alignment of menhirs at Parc-y-Meirw, Pembrokeshire, W 9/7, SM 999359 (51° 59'·2, 4° 54'·9).

1965) with a sea horizon. Later the 1-in Ordnance Survey of Ireland was consulted and it was found that Mount Leinster and some surrounding ground are always above the sea horizon on this azimuth (Fig. 6.19). Since the distance is 91 miles it seems that the atmosphere was clearer in Megalithic times than it is today. It is only in the Hebrides that I have been able to obtain sights of this kind of length. I visited Mid Clyth many times before I got the 50-mile sight I needed there (Chapter 9).

The distance and the consequent low altitude make it impossible to be certain of the value of either terrestrial or astronomical refraction. The profile shown has been calculated using (3.7), but the uncertainty in the altitudes may amount to several minutes, and in fact the variations to be expected from day to day may be considerable. In the present state of our knowledge it is unsafe to assume that Croaghaun would have been visible on the Moon's disc, but it seems reasonable to assume that the point A was normally visible.

7

AN ANALYSIS OF THE OBSERVED DECLINATIONS

7.1. IN this chapter we shall deduce the mean values of ϵ, i, Δ, s, and parallax that best suit the declinations of what are considered to be the most reliable foresights. These foresights are marked on the profiles by A or where there are more than one by A, A_1, A_2, etc.

The particulars for all these forty points are collected in Table 7.1. Table 7.2 contains lines to which, for one reason or another, either no weight or no precision can be attached. For example, while the orientation of the stone at Knockstaple, A 4/19, shows that this line is lunar, we cannot say which point on the profile was intended. On some of the profiles, while one or more points are definite and have been accepted, others marked B seem to be uncertain. The B lines have been tabulated to widen the overall picture of the known sites.

The altitudes tabulated under h were corrected by applying night-time refraction from Table 3.1 and parallax $= 57' \cdot 0$. The declination in the next column was then found by using (2.5). If we are really dealing with lunar lines we expect that each declination will be one of the values of $\pm(\epsilon \pm i \pm \Delta \pm s)$, where Δ, the perturbation, may be zero. The combination of ϵ, i, Δ, and s appropriate to each declination is given in the next column. It is permissible to put $s = 0$ only where there is sufficient room for side movement to get both limbs.

The sign of s shows which limb was used. A short examination shows that there was no preference; the lower limb was used as often as the upper. Fig. 10.1 of Thom 1967 shows the same thing, but there no attempt was made to remove the perturbation before the histogram was plotted. But the number of lines for the setting Moon ($360° >$ azimuth $> 180°$) is double that for the rising Moon ($180° >$ azimuth $> 0°$). This preference probably arose because the rising Moon appears suddenly and the twinkle of the limb in a notch may be missed, whereas it is easy to follow a setting body down to the horizon. There seems to be a slight preference for south declinations. Perhaps the explanation is that at its furthest south the *full* Moon is well placed for observation in the summer and the bleak position of some of the sites may have made this an important consideration. It should be remembered that for a few days near new Moon observation is not possible.

Table 7.1. *The forty lines chosen for analysis*

Site	Fig.	Point	Az.	h	δ	
H 3/11	6.3	A_2	157° 16′	−10′·5	−29° 29′·5	$-(\epsilon+i+\Delta+s)$
H 1/1	6.13	A_2	189 52	+75 ·8	−29 27 ·1	$-(\epsilon+i+\Delta+s)$
M 1/3	6.12	A	189 56	+161 ·0	−29 26 ·9	$-(\epsilon+i+\Delta+s)$
N 1/1	9.3	A_2	160 5	−11 ·0	−29 26 ·6	$-(\epsilon+i+\Delta+s)$
A 4/2	6.2	A_1	156 12	+77 ·0	−29 26 ·4	$-(\epsilon+i+\Delta+s)$
H 1/5	6.14	A_3	168 30	68 ·0	−29 26 ·3	$-(\epsilon+i+\Delta+s)$
A 6/4	6.10	A	204 0	55 ·0	−29 25 ·9	$-(\epsilon+i+\Delta+s)$
A 4/14	6.4	A_2	177 48	291 ·7	−28 53 ·8	$-(\epsilon+i+\Delta-s)$
P 3/1	6.16	—	197 57	118 ·0	−28 55	$-(\epsilon+i+\Delta-s)$
H 1/5	6.14	A_2	164 40	64 ·5	−28 58 ·1	$-(\epsilon+i+\Delta+s)$
H 1/5	6.14	A_4	170 20	84 ·3	−29 20 ·5	$-(\epsilon+i+0+s)$
N 1/17	9.5	A_1	191 54	59 ·0	−29 19 ·1	$-(\epsilon+i+0+s)$
A 2/8	5.1	A_2	207 56	18 ·0	−28 48	$-(\epsilon+i+0-s)$
A 4/2	6.2	A_2	152 30	57 ·0	−28 45 ·7	$-(\epsilon+i+0-s)$
A 4/14	6.4	A_1	177 26	300 ·6	−28 44 ·0	$-(\epsilon+i+0-s)$
N 1/17	9.5	A_2	194 25	68 ·0	−28 48 ·5	$-(\epsilon+i+0-s)$
H 1/1	6.13	A_1	188 45	+95 ·8	−29 11 ·6	$-(\epsilon+i-\Delta+s)$
N 1/1	9.3	A_1	158 30	−13 ·0	−29 8 ·7	$-(\epsilon+i-\Delta+s)$
H 3/11	6.15	A_1	155 35	−10 ·5	−29 4 ·6	$-(\epsilon+i-\Delta+s)$
A 4/1	6.1	A	207 17	+49 ·0	−28 39 ·3	$-(\epsilon+i-\Delta-s)$
A 4/9	5.6	A_2	211 20	−4 ·0	−28 37 ·3	$-(\epsilon+i-\Delta-s)$
H 1/5	6.14	A_1	162 40	+66 ·5	−28 35 ·4	$-(\epsilon+i-\Delta-s)$
A 2/5	4.4	A_2	232 45	39 ·0	−18 40 ·6	$-(\epsilon-i+\Delta-s)$
P 4/1	5.5	A	126 49	8 ·0	−18 59 ·7	$-(\epsilon-i+0+s)$
A 2/5	4.4	A_1	233 23	+41 ·5	−18 20 ·3	$-(\epsilon-i-\Delta-s)$
G 3/2	6.17	A_2	303 28	−25 ·0	+18 17 ·8	$+(\epsilon-i-\Delta-s)$
A 4/9	5.6	A_1	303 0	+2 ·0	+18 18 ·0	$+(\epsilon-i-\Delta-s)$
W 9/7	6.19	A	300 50	−21 ·6	+18 19 ·7	$+(\epsilon-i-\Delta-s)$
G 3/2	6.17	A_1	304 25	−4 ·0	+19 9 ·9	$+(\epsilon-i+\Delta+s)$
A 4/5	6.3	A	326 38	+39 ·0	+29 12 ·0	$+(\epsilon+i-\Delta+s)$
A 2/12	5.3	A_1	321 30	176 ·0	+29 13 ·6	$+(\epsilon+i+\Delta+0)$
A 4/17	6.5	A	323 45	67 ·0	+28 34 ·6	$+(\epsilon+i-\Delta-s)$
P 1/10	5.4	A	30 55	34 ·0	+29 18 ·8	$+(\epsilon+i+0+s)$
A 2/13	6.8	A	324 59	98 ·0	+29 17 ·0	$+(\epsilon+i+0+s)$
A 2/12	5.3	A_2	322 13	174 ·0	+29 28 ·5	$+(\epsilon+i+\Delta+s)$
A 4/17	6.5	A_2	34 15	74 ·0	+29 26 ·3	$+(\epsilon+i+\Delta+s)$
A 10/5	6.11	A	326 0	45 ·0	+28 54 ·2	$+(\epsilon+i+\Delta-s)$
A 2/8	5.1	A_1 from S_1	316 59 ·0	277 ·7	+28 56 ·5	$+(\epsilon+i+\Delta-s)$
A 2/8	5.1	A_1 from S_5	317 52 ·5	277 ·2	+29 19 ·1	$+(\epsilon+i+0+s)$
A 2/8	5.1	A_1 from Q	317 12 ·6	277 ·7	+29 2 ·5	$+(\epsilon+i+0+0)$

Table 7.2. *Lines with either low weight or low precision*

Site		Point	Az.	h	δ	
P 4/1	Lundin Links	B	234° 14′	+19′	−18° 19′	$-(\epsilon-i-\Delta-s)$
A 2/13	Dunadd	B	323 25	99	+28 44	$+(\epsilon+i-s)$
A 4/19	Knockstaple	B	326 09	20	+28 54	$+(\epsilon+i+\Delta-s)$
A 6/1	Camus an Stacca	B	198 20	159	−28 58	$-(\epsilon+i+\Delta-s)$
A 6/1	Camus an Stacca	B	199 30	163	−28 39	$-(\epsilon+i-\Delta-s)$
M 1/3	Quinish	B	197 00	142	−28 45	$-(\epsilon+i+0-s)$
G 3/2	Haggstone	B	304 38	−21	+18 58	$+(\epsilon-i+0+s)$
G 3/2	Haggstone	B	303 38	−20	+18 29	$+(\epsilon-i+0-s)$
L 1/16	Blakeley Moss	B	325 12	−2	+28 46	$+(\epsilon+i+0-s)$
P 1/10	Fowlis Wester	B	30 22	35	+29 31	$+(\epsilon+i+\Delta+s)$
A 2/8	Temple Wood	B	203 46	52	−29 19	$+(\epsilon+i+0+s)$
G 9/13	Kell B.		129 50	99	−19 04	$-(\epsilon-i+0+s)$

7.2. For those who prefer a pictorial representation Fig. 7.1 has been plotted. Neglecting sign, the differences between the declinations in Table 7.1 and the appropriate value of $\pm(\epsilon\pm i)$ were found. In the figure each of these differences is plotted as a small Gaussian area. When these areas are added we get a kind of histogram. We expect values at 0, $s-\Delta$, s, and $s+\Delta$. Clumps occur at all these values except the first. In fact the only two values

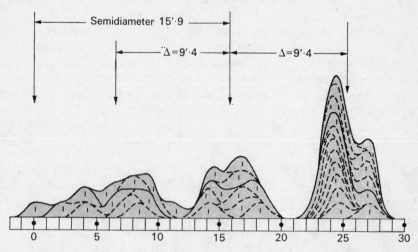

FIG. 7.1. Histogram of difference between the observed declination and $\pm(\epsilon\pm i)$.

near zero come from two of the most important sites, namely Temple Wood and Ballymeanach, both of which have a line for the Moon's centre with zero perturbation. The histogram is definite enough to make a formal statistical analysis desirable, and this will now be given.

7.3. The first analysis

The top line of Table 7.1 allows us to write

$$-29°·492 = -\epsilon-i-\Delta-s, \tag{7.1}$$

and so with every entry. We thus have forty 'observation equations' for the four unknowns. By the usual method of least squares these are reduced to the four 'normal equations',

$$1090·78 = 40\epsilon+26i+ 5\Delta+ 2s, \tag{7.2}$$
$$830·60 = 26\epsilon+40i+ 9\Delta+ 8s,$$
$$172·44 = 5\epsilon+ 9i+29\Delta+ 8s,$$
$$100·30 = 2\epsilon+ 8i+ 8\Delta+38s.$$

Solving these gives $\qquad\qquad \epsilon = 23° \, 53' \, 26''$, $\qquad\qquad\qquad$ (7.3)

$$i = \ 5° \ 8' \, 52'',$$

$$\Delta = \qquad 9' \, 23'',$$

$$s = \qquad 15' \, 55''.$$

The value of i, the inclination of the lunar orbit, agrees closely with the astronomer's value, namely $5° \, 8' \, 43''$. Similarly the value of the perturbation is much what we expect, but the semidiameter is interesting. As has already been explained, this can vary throughout the month from about $14'·7$ to $16'·7$ with a time mean of $15' \, 32''$. This mean value might have been substituted in the observation equations, thereby reducing the number of unknowns to three, but it is much more interesting to see how nearly the value found above agrees with the known mean.

7.4. The second analysis

Another quantity which varies throughout the month is parallax, the limits being about $53'·9$ and $61'·5$ with a time mean of $57' \, 3''$. In a study of how these people worked, it is important to know if their foresights show a maximum or a mean parallax. It is difficult to separate the effects of parallax and refraction. Both act on the altitude and so on the declination. An increase of altitude of amount b always produces a positive increase in declination of amount $b \, d\delta/dh$. The fact that this is algebraically positive and that we have both positive and negative declinations allows the total effect of refraction and parallax to be determined. Only if we had a large sample of accurate lines covering a wide range of altitude would it be possible to effect a complete separation. An example of how refraction, both terrestrial and astronomical, can thus be determined from the sites themselves will be found in Thom 1969. It was this investigation that showed that much better consistency resulted if higher values for both types of refraction were used.

Here we shall adopt a simpler method. Provided the altitude is greater than a degree or two the refraction is sufficiently certain to ensure that it introduces no serious error. We shall now accordingly use only those lines with altitudes greater than $1°$. In calculating the declinations we used a parallax of $57'$. Let us now take $57' + \pi$, where π is to be determined from the sight lines. The geocentric altitude to be used in calculating the declination is now increased by π, so that the declination is increased by $\pi \, d\delta/dh$. The factor $d\delta/dh$ for our lines lies between $0·91$ and $1·00$. In view of the other uncertainties it is sufficient to put it equal to unity. A more elaborate calculation using the correct values showed practically an identical final result. It so happens that none of these lines with high altitudes is for the minor standstill $(\epsilon - i)$. Hence we can only solve for $(\epsilon + i)$, which we shall write E.

Take the semidiameter as $0°·260$. Then the second item in Table 7.1 yields the equation

$$-29°·452+\pi = -(\epsilon+i)-\Delta-0°·260,$$

or, changing sign, $\qquad 29°·192 = E+\Delta+\pi.$ \hfill (7.4)

As a typical *north* declination line take A 4/17, which yields

$$28°·837 = E-\Delta-\pi. \hfill (7.5)$$

There are altogether twenty such lines, and since some are for north declinations and some for south the difference in the sign of π allows this quantity to be determined. Since we propose to solve for the three unknowns E, Δ, and π, we again use 'least squares', and eventually find

$$E = 29° 2' 16'', \qquad \Delta = 9' 55'', \quad \text{and} \quad \pi = -5''. \hfill (7.6)$$

The very small value obtained for π is of course fortuitous. A repeat calculation using only the eight lines with altitudes greater than $2\frac{1}{2}°$ showed

$$E = 29° 1' 19'', \qquad \Delta = 10' 16'', \quad \text{and} \quad \pi = -1' 26''. \hfill (7.7)$$

These small values show that, as with the semidiameter, we obtain a mean value for parallax. This is of course a statistical conclusion, but we have seen earlier that the elaborate and precise observatory at Temple Wood taken by itself shows a parallax not much different from the mean.

These results may be summarized by saying that the forty lines of Table 7.1 are best represented by an obliquity of $23° 53'·4$ and values of i, Δ, s, and p very close to modern mean values. This value of ϵ corresponds to a mean date of 1650 B.C. This date is later than that found for Temple Wood itself, but, as we shall see, the accuracies of the determinations are not nearly sufficient to warrant saying that Temple Wood is necessarily earlier than the other sites.

One possible criticism of the above value of ϵ is that a small error may be present if there was a tendency to observe south declinations in the summer and north declinations in the winter. The lower summer refraction would increase numerically the declination and therefore ϵ. Similarly the higher winter refraction acts on the north declinations to increase them also. But we can look at the result from the twenty lines with higher altitudes and therefore less refraction. Here $E = 29° 2' 16''$ and so, deducting i, $\epsilon = 23° 53' 33''$, agreeing closely with the over-all result. Another complication is discussed in the next paragraph.

7.5. Effect of parallax changes

We must not overlook the manner in which parallax can affect the conclusions regarding the sites. We have throughout used a mean parallax of $p = 57'·0$, corresponding to the mean distance of the Moon from the Earth. Let us assume that when the Moon is nearest to the Earth, that is at perigee, the parallax is $p+\Delta p$ and that when it is at apogee parallax is $p-\Delta p$. The interval separating two observing times, i.e. two declination maxima, is the tropical month (see Appendix A), which has a mean length of 27·32159 days; and the interval between two passages of the Moon through perigee is the anomalistic month of 27·55455 days. Note that these do not differ by as much as a quarter of a day. Now suppose that perigee happened at a declination maximum near the standstill. Parallax would be $p+\Delta p$, and at the next declination maximum, a tropical month later, it would be practically the same. In fact for several months parallax would be near its maximum when the Moon was on a foresight for $+(\epsilon+i)$, but a fortnight later, when the Moon was on the foresight for $-(\epsilon+i)$, parallax would be at its minimum $p-\Delta p$.

What effect can this have on our conclusions? A serious case would arise if an observatory like Temple Wood had been erected by observations made at a single standstill like that just described. To show how serious it could be, consider such an observatory with a foresight in the north for $+(\epsilon+i)$ and one in the south for $-(\epsilon+i)$. Assume that we, today, measure up the foresights and calculate the declinations without applying parallax, obtaining δ_N and $-\delta_S$. We ought to apply parallax of $p+\Delta p$ to the north lines and $p-\Delta p$ to the south. When we do, we obtain for the declinations

$$\delta_N+(p+\Delta p)\mathrm{d}\delta/\mathrm{d}h \text{ and } -\delta_S+(p-\Delta p)\mathrm{d}\delta/\mathrm{d}h.$$

Both of these should give $(\epsilon+i)$, and so

$$(\epsilon+i) = \delta_N+(p+\Delta p)\mathrm{d}\delta/\mathrm{d}h \tag{7.8}$$

and

$$-(\epsilon+i) = -\delta_S+(p-\Delta p)\mathrm{d}\delta/\mathrm{d}h.$$

Solving for p and Δp we obtain

$$2p\,\mathrm{d}\delta/\mathrm{d}h = \delta_S-\delta_N \tag{7.9}$$

and

$$2\Delta p\,\mathrm{d}\delta/\mathrm{d}h = 2(\epsilon+i)-(\delta_N+\delta_S). \tag{7.10}$$

For present purposes $\mathrm{d}\delta/\mathrm{d}h$ may be taken as unity. The expression (7.9) tells us what has already been explained, namely, that such an observatory allows the *mean* parallax p to be deduced from the two foresights, and (7.10) tells us that the foresights by themselves cannot provide values of Δp and $(\epsilon+i)$. If we assume, as we have done hitherto, that Δp is zero, than $(\epsilon+i)$ can be found, but to determine Δp we must know $(\epsilon+i)$.

It is most unlikely that Temple Wood was built at a single standstill, but the above shows that it does not seem possible to deduce this from the internal evidence. It is here that the solstitial sites help us. The obliquity found from them in Chapter 4 is 23° 54'·2, that found at Temple Wood itself in Chapter 5 is 23° 53'·8 (§ 5.4), and that found in this chapter by considering a large number of sites is 23° 53'·4. We might explain the similarity of these values by saying that all the sites were erected about the same time, i.e. at a time when it so happened that parallax was at its mean value when the Moon was at its maximum declination. The alternative and much more likely explanation is that erection was spread over a long period of time and the stones were placed to mark mean values. An estimate of the minimum length of the period of time is 93 years. This is based on the values given in Table 7.3, which makes

Table 7.3. *The relation of perigee to the declination maximum*

Number of standstills	1	2	3	4	5	6
Corresponding no. of days	6798	13 596	20 394	27 191	33 989	40 787
No. of tropical months	249	498	747	995	1244	1493
I_1 = corresponding no. of days	6803	13 606	20 409	27 185	33 988	40 791
Number of anomalistic months	247	494	741	987	1234	1481
I_2 = corresponding no. of days	6806	13 612	20 418	27 196	34 002	40 808
Difference = $I_2 - I_1$	3	6	9	11	14	17

use of the lengths of the tropical and anomalistic months given in Appendix A. Assume that at a certain standstill it so happened that the declination maximum and perigee (the parallax maximum) occurred on the same day. Table 7.3 shows that the next standstill would be about 6798 days later and that in this time there would have been 249 tropical months lasting 6803 days and 247 anomalistic months lasting 6806 days. Thus the parallax maximum would have happened 3 days after the declination maximum. This interval would have increased progressively with each standstill, until at the fifth, i.e. after 33 989 days or about 93 years, it would have been 14 days or about half a period. Then, and not before, would a parallax *minimum* have occurred *at a declination maximum at a standstill.*

Let us look at some actual values. We see from Fig. 2.3 that there was a standstill at A.D. 1969·22. Working back from this with a mean interval of 18·6126 years (Table 1, Appendix A) we find that a standstill occurred at 1716·07 B.C. There was a declination maximum at 1969·231, and working back from this with multiples of the tropical month we find a declination maximum at 1716·063 B.C. Similarly using the anomalistic month from a known perigee we find that perigee occurred at 1716·064 B.C. Note that these three dates are within a day or two of one another, which means that at this standstill parallax was a maximum when the declination was a maximum. Fig. 7.2 shows the values of parallax at the observing times from 1800 B.C. to 1500 B.C. Observations must have been made on a number of nights at each standstill so it will never be possible to calculate exact values of the parallax; it would be slightly different on each night. Nevertheless Fig. 7.2 is not without interest. For example, if a given observatory had been established as a result of observations made at the standstill in 1660 B.C., we should find there mean parallax for the north and south declinations. But the same thing would happen if the observations had been spread over the standstills from 1716 to 1623 B.C.

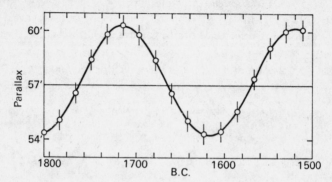

FIG. 7.2. Moon's parallax at the north declination maxima at the major standstills from 1800 to 1500 B.C.

Whatever span archaeologists eventually allot to the megalith builders, it is unlikely to be less than 93 years. It follows that the majority of the stones were almost certainly erected to show mean values over a long period of years. This fits in with the kind of backsights we find at the lunar observatories: large stones set up to last. Further work along these lines at other observatories is obviously desirable, but what is really needed is for the dates of the sites to be reliably established by some other independent method. It remains to be seen if a method of sufficient accuracy can be developed by archaeologists.

In reading this chapter confusion will result unless the reader is clear about the difference between the angles we have written as π and Δp. The first, π, is an increment to the known value of mean parallax, $57'\cdot 0$. On theoretical grounds we should expect to find it to be zero by measurements at the sites, and it has been shown how accurately the more reliable sight lines do give this value. On the other hand, Δp may or may not be zero. It will change sign in a fortnight, and can only be found from the sites if we already know ϵ by some independent means.

8

EXTRAPOLATION THEORY

8.1. AT several places in Caithness we find peculiar fan-like arrangements of stones. In 1871 Sir H. Dryden made surveys of most of these sites, but unfortunately his method of surveying was so crude that his diagrams are only useful in showing the number of stones that were still in place 100 years ago. No satisfactory explanation of these stone rows has so far been put forward, but recently, when studying methods of extrapolation that might have been available at the Megalithic lunar observatories, I found I had developed a geometrical method that corresponds exactly with what is found in the Caithness rows. There are not enough complete examples in existence to make possible a statistical assessment of the probability that these rows were designed for making the necessary extrapolation at the sites, but some form of extrapolation was necessary (otherwise we cannot explain what we find), and there, still lying beside the observing positions, are the necessary instruments. If the stone rows were not for extrapolation then why do we find them beside or near obvious backsights for lunar observations?

Before proceeding to study the exposition of how the extrapolation was done, it is necessary to have a clear understanding of the observing method described in Chapter 1.

8.2. Finding the lunation maximum

Before the erectors could have obtained the kind of accuracy we find, for example, at Temple Wood, there were serious difficulties to be overcome. In this chapter we shall deal with one of the greatest obstacles to accuracy, and show what seems to have been the method of overcoming it. The reader will then be in a position to assess the evidence that advanced methods of this kind were in use.

There are two separate problems. How were the sites originally set out, and how were they used?

When a modern astronomer orders, for example, a new transit instrument, he expects a long delay before it is designed, made, and erected, and before he gets it into final adjustment. But once this is completed he expects to be able to use it regularly without long delays in getting results. So it must have been with the completed observatories of Megalithic man. Years of patient work must have gone into finding a suitable site, marking the backsights, and laying out the ancillary gear, which, as we shall see, in some places still exists. But once the observatory was complete one would expect it to work smoothly and efficiently. The analogy becomes more convincing when we remember that there are remains of many of these observatories throughout Britain. The builders had plenty of experience and knew what they were doing.

The great difficulty that faced these people was that observations could be made only once a day when the Moon was on the horizon and only occasionally would moonset or moonrise occur at the instant when the declination was a maximum. In Fig. 8.1 we see the kind of thing that happens to the

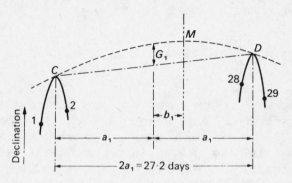

FIG. 8.1. Two successive maxima.

Moon's declination during one lunation. On the first and second days of the month the declination at, for example, moonset might be as shown at 1 and 2. Then until the twenty-eighth the declination remains too low to be shown on this figure or indeed to be seen from anywhere near the foresight in use. If the declinations on the first and second happen to be nearly equal then both will be, as we have seen in Chapter 3, about 12' below the maximum, an impermissible error. It is true that the observer might go on working for a lifetime until he had the absolute maximum. This kind of thing would have been undesirable during the erection, but intolerable during the use of the observatory, and would indeed have rendered the whole project useless. We must also bear in mind that at Temple Wood not only is the $\epsilon+i+\Delta$ case recorded, but marks are there also for $\epsilon+i$ and elsewhere for $\epsilon+i-\Delta$, and that these have apparently been established for *mean* parallax and semi-diameter and for mean perturbation Δ. The only possible conclusion is that some method existed whereby the process could be speeded up. In other words, the builders of the sites must have had some method of extrapolating from the stake positions obtained by two or three nights' observation to obtain the position for the maximum declination for that lunation. If they could solve the problem involved in this they were well on the way to finding the time of maximum, minimum, or node of the 9' perturbation and so the times of the eclipse danger periods. They were also in a position to be able to make a study of the anomalies that they knew to exist and were probably trying to sort out.

8.3. For our present study of their methods it is sufficiently accurate to write the declination deficiency for the monthly wave as kt^2, where t is the time in days before or after the maximum and k has the value given in § 2.7, namely 46·5 at a major standstill and 30·0 at a minor. The mean interval between two successive settings of the Moon is 1·0350 days, conveniently thought of as a lunar day. At a major standstill half a lunar day after the declination maximum the declination deficiency is

$$kt^2 = 46·0(1·0350 \times \tfrac{1}{2})^2 = 12'·3. \tag{8.1}$$

It follows that if it so happens that the maximum occurs midway in time between two successive risings of the Moon the declination deficiency on both occasions will be 12'·3.

Megalithic man could not know or measure (as we understand measure) this angle, but what he could and apparently did know at the important sites, and perhaps at all sites, was the corresponding distance (G) on the ground. He would have found this distance experimentally by some empirical method (§ 9.6), but for comparison with his values we shall find it at the various sites by calculation.

To produce a declination change of kt^2 requires an azimuth change of $\Delta A = kt^2 \, dA/d\delta$ minutes. Assuming that the ground is level so that a side shift does not change the altitude, the distance the observer has to move to the side to produce this change of azimuth is $D \times \Delta A/3438$, D being the distance to the foresight and 3438 the number of minutes in a radian. It is convenient to write this as Kt^2. Thus if D is in miles we obtain

$$y = Kt^2 = Dkt^2 \, dA/d\delta \times 5280/3438 \text{ (feet)} \tag{8.2}$$

as the equation of the parabolic curve shown on the ground in Fig. 1.1.

We think of the time t in days as being plotted at right angles to the line of movement AA (Fig. 1.1), and the origin as being between W and Th.

We define G as the stake movement corresponding to the declination deficiency half a lunar day before or after the maximum. Thus we find at the major standstill (taking kt^2 from (8.1)) the expression for this very important length:

Major standstill $\quad G = 12·3 \, D \, dA/d\delta \times 5280/3438$

$$= 18·9 \, D \, dA/d\delta \text{ (feet)}. \tag{8.3}$$

Similarly at the minor standstill we find

$$G = 12·2 \, D \, dA/d\delta. \tag{8.4}$$

We can calculate $dA/d\delta$ by taking the reciprocal of $d\delta/dA$ as given by (2.7). Since the above expressions involve the second power of t the movement for a whole lunar day is $4G$.

For the non-mathematical reader we may explain wherein lies the importance of the length G that we find recorded at some of the sites. If on two successive nights the observer finds the same stake position, all he has to do to get the position corresponding to the maximum declination *at that lunation* is to move to the side a distance G. If, on the other hand, he finds the stakes were $4G$ apart then one of them is already in the maximum position. This greatly increased the usefulness of the observatory, but what did he do if the stakes, while being not exactly in the same place, were not far apart? He would naturally move a distance G from the point midway between the stakes, and this as we shall see is a close approximation.

He perhaps went on using some such method until he realized that to move G from the mid-position failed to give accuracy when the distance between the stakes was large. It was obvious that when the distance between the stakes approached its maximum $4G$ the movement was nearer $2G$ than G. Accordingly he tried to devise some method of correction, the correction necessary remaining small for low values of the distance between the stakes, but rising more and more rapidly for large values.

That the problem was solved and a method evolved is shown by the evidence at Mid Clyth and elsewhere. We do not know the reasoning which led to this solution, but, knowing something of their other geometrical achievements and their tenacity of purpose, need we be surprised that these people were ultimately successful? Given determination, time, and freedom from distraction, there was perhaps nothing to prevent them developing a method of this kind empirically.

We shall give a mathematical demonstration, but this gives no more than a hint as to how the genius who was ultimately responsible knew that his solution was in theory correct.

8.4. How would a scientist of today solve the problem?

We shall now show how a person with a knowledge of elementary mathematics could solve the problem, which may be stated thus: Given two stake positions one placed before and one, a day later, after the maximum, to find how to extrapolate to the stake position for the maximum at that lunation, assuming G to be known.

We shall demonstrate by using the parabola $y = Kt^2$, which would be obtained on the ground by moving back along the line of sight a small constant distance each night. It need not be assumed that Megalithic man made this backward movement. It is introduced here to simplify the demonstration, which otherwise becomes entirely algebraic.

In Fig. 8.2 the line of movement with no stepping back is shown on the right at *MLCR*. The same lettering is used for corresponding points in the opened-out presentation on the left. L and R are the stake positions on two successive nights, y_L and y_R being the deficiencies. We seek to find M, but

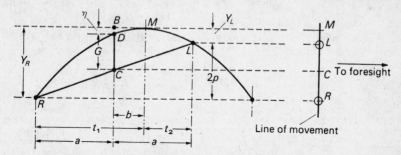

FIG. 8.2. Finding η from the observed movement $2p$. Note that R is the stake on the observer's right and L on his left.

till we know its position we do not know y_L or y_R. We do know the distance between L and R, i.e. $y_R - y_L$. We shall call this distance $2p$, so that

$$2p = y_R - y_L. \tag{8.5}$$

The first stake R has been placed at a time t_1 (unknown) before the maximum and the second a lunar day later $(2a)$, i.e. t_2 after the maximum. Put $b = $ time interval between the instant in time midway between the observations and the maximum. Then from Fig. 8.2 $t_1 = a+b$ and $t_2 = a-b$. Since $y = Kt^2$ we have

$$y_R = Kt_1^2 = K(a+b)^2 = K(a^2+2ab+b^2), \tag{8.6}$$

$$y_L = Kt_2^2 = K(a-b)^2 = K(a^2-2ab+b^2). \tag{8.7}$$

We shall now show that the sagitta DC is equal to G. We have $DC = BC - BD = \frac{1}{2}(y_L+y_R)-Kb^2$. On substituting values from (8.6) and (8.7) this becomes simply Ka^2. But Ka^2 is the deficiency half a lunar day (a) before or after the maximum, which we have called G. Thus the sagitta is constant and always equal to G.

We see that if the observer moved to his left a distance G from C, the point midway between the stakes R and L, he was short of the maximum M by BD, a distance which we shall call η. This distance is small provided the distance $2p$ between the stakes is small. But from (8.5) $2p = y_L - y_R$, which becomes, when we substitute values from (8.6) and (8.7), simply $4Kab$. That is,

$$2p = 4Kab, \quad \text{or} \quad b = p/2Ka, \tag{8.8}$$

and η, which is Kb^2, can be written $p^2/4Ka^2$. But we have seen that G is always Ka^2, and therefore finally

$$\eta = p^2/4G. \tag{8.9}$$

Thus, knowing $2p$ and G, we move to the left from the midpoint C a total distance $G+p^2/4G$ to get the position for the maximum.

In this form a little arithmetic is required to find η, but it is easy to obtain a geometrical substitute. Lay out a distance AB (Fig. 8.3) of length $4G$, and at B erect a perpendicular BC of length p. Join A and C. Then by similar triangles the offset at D, distant p from A, is $p^2/4G$, which is the required value of η. In some places we find a length very nearly $4G$ laid out on flat ground.

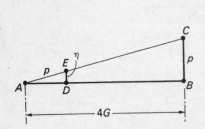

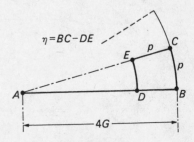

FIG. 8.3. The triangle method of extrapolation.

FIG. 8.4. The sector method of extrapolation.

Ranging rods could be placed at D and E, a second person sighting from A to B and C. As we shall see, this was probably the method used in Argyllshire. In Caithness a modification of the same idea was used. This is shown in Fig. 8.4. Here η is obviously the difference between BC and DE. In Caithness we find sites where a fan-like sector of stone rows radiating from an unmarked centre is laid out on the ground ready for use. Ranging rods are unnecessary. One man can use the computer alone without the need for an assistant to sight from the centre, which in two sites is not visible as it is on lower ground.

These grids of stones had a second use, which enhanced their value and also allowed a reduction in size. This second method was used when $2p$ was greater than $2G$. It is true that the first method described above applies to any value of $2p$. But as $2p$ approaches $4G$ the distance y_L approaches zero. It would be convenient to be able to find y_L directly so that this distance, i.e. LM in Fig. 8.2 (right), could be measured from the most advanced, L, of the two stakes, to give M the maximum.

Write
$$m = 2G-p. \tag{8.10}$$

Then
$$m^2/4G = (4G^2-4Gp+p^2)/4G = G-p+p^2/4G$$
$$= G-p+\eta.$$

But from the figure $y_L = MC-LC = G+\eta-p$, which is $m^2/4G$.

Hence
$$y_L = m^2/4G. \tag{8.11}$$

Comparing this with (8.8), we see that the same geometrical construction that was used for finding η from p can also be used for finding y_L from m. The advantage of being able to use either y_L or η is obvious; the size of grid necessary is halved. When p is less than G use (8.9); when it is greater than G use (8.11). This explains why the main sector at Mid Clyth has a base and a height of exactly G.

8.5. Finding the date of the maximum, first method

We can use the theory developed above in an entirely different way. Above it was used to find the stake position for M at one lunation. Suppose we have found three successive such stake positions at three successive lunations. These now correspond to C, D, and E, or U, V, and W in Fig. 2.3. The problem is, given three such stakes, can we deduce the date of the intermediate maximum? Imagine that, for example, U, V, and W are represented in Fig. 8.2 by R, D, and L. Now a is a month instead of half a day, and the time interval b is the time by which C is before the maximum, i.e. the interval we have to add to the date of V to obtain the date of the maximum.

From (8.8) b is equal to $p/2Ka$, which is $pa/2G$. We need a new G, but the important thing is that the required interval b is proportional to the distance $(2p)$ between the stakes for U and W. Perhaps this is obvious, but it is as well to have it established rigorously. To use this method the observer has to know very simply that for every x yards in the distance between the stakes for U and W the date of V is one day before the maximum. It was particularly easy to find x by taking advantage of any occasion on which two successive stakes were found to be in the same place or almost so. The date of the maximum was obvious and the distance to the third stake allowed x to be found.

This method does not need a predetermined backsight, but a stone set up for $(\epsilon+i+\Delta)$ would ensure that the maximum being used was sufficiently near the standstill. This may account for the large number of stones we find for the extreme declination.

8.6. Finding the date of the maximum, second method

While the above method may have been extensively used, there was another method available. Referring again to Fig. 2.3, suppose that stakes have been placed for B, C, E, and F. Then, with sufficient accuracy, linear interpolation could be used to find the dates N and M when the perturbation was zero or nearly zero.

This method presupposes that a permanent backsight existed for $(\epsilon+i)$. As we saw in Chapter 5, highly developed observatories like Temple Wood have backsights accurately placed for both $+(\epsilon+i)$ and $-(\epsilon+i)$, indicating perhaps that this was considered to be the most reliable method. The time interval between N and M is on the average one-half of the period, or 87 days, but at standstills when parallax was large we can be sure that observers would not fail to notice the association between the consequent shorter interval and the lower position of the maximum.

Both methods require that the necessary stakes be placed by using an extrapolation method, and so we see that there was no escaping the necessity of having at any observatory the requisite ancillary layout. Dependent as all the observatories were on observations made of necessity only once a day, they were useless without this equipment. If we assume that they were scientific institutions built to study the movements of the Moon, the necessity was all the greater.

9

THE STONE ROWS AND THEIR USE

9.1. WE find parallel rows of stones in various parts of Britain, but the fan-shaped sectors of rows are peculiar to Caithness. These rows consist mostly of small stones or slabs set on edge with the long axis along the row. The stones are seldom more than 1½ feet high and are very often so low as to be invisible in the vegetation. This makes the sites difficult to find, and once found, hours of prodding with a bayonet or a steel rod may be necessary to locate enough definite stones to make a pattern. At Garrywhin (Thom 1964, fig. 2) I have so far failed to find enough to be able to fit a convincing sector to the plan and do not propose to discuss this site further.

In 1871 Sir H. Dryden measured up most of the known sites. Although his method of surveying was crude and his plans are of little use by themselves, they do show what was there a century ago. I suspect that, except at Mid Clyth where he shows some 248 stones, the stones he found are still there, but more deeply buried than in his time. A danger in prodding is that one tends to move along a suspected line and find 'stones' that are simply the stony ground on which the site is built. One wonders if some of Dryden's crosses, marking stones 'felt', are spurious. Of the four sites dealt with here only one, Loch of Yarrows, is in a position likely to have been disturbed by cultivation, but the most important of all at Mid Clyth has been disturbed by a quarry and certainly has been raided for building material.

It should be said that the only other multiple-row site I have succeeded in finding in Caithness is that near Dunreay. It seems to consist of parallel rows and does not appear to have any bearing on the present subject (Thom 1964, fig. 3), but it may of course be some undeciphered method of extrapolation.

We shall now discuss the four sites where there are rows radiating with a definite or fairly definite radius.

9.2. The Hill o' Many Stanes, Mid Clyth, N 1/1, ND 296384

Fig. 9.1 shows a small-scale reproduction of a careful survey with, superimposed, the suggested geometrical construction used for setting out the rows. A statistical analysis will be found in Thom 1964. This shows conclusively that the stones were intended to be on a grid of uniformly spaced arcs and radial lines. There are three or four stones still in place to the east of the main

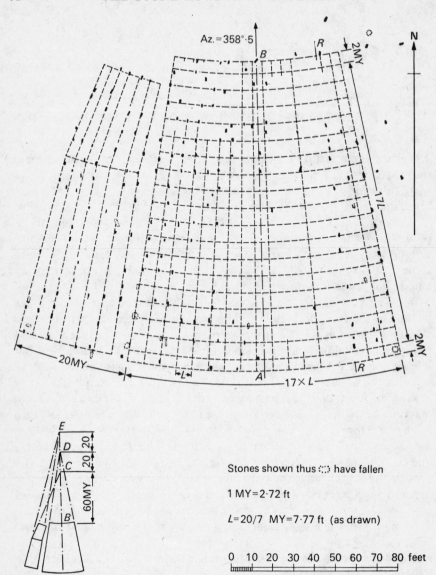

Az.=358°·5

Stones shown thus ⸬ have fallen

1 MY=2·72 ft

L=20/7 MY=7·77 ft (as drawn)

0   10 20 30 40 50 60 70 80 feet

FIG. 9.1. Mid Clyth, N 1/1, showing layout of sectors.

sector, which may be taken as an indication that there were annexes there symmetrical with those on the west. If this idea is correct, the most easterly line at its top end would have had an azimuth of nearly 160° and so would have pointed to the hills shown in Fig. 9.2. The profile of these hills was calculated as accurately as possible from the 1-in O.S., using (3.7) for the altitudes. Later an opportunity presented itself of seeing these hills from Mid Clyth, although the distances are about 50 miles. The measurements then taken are also shown on the figure. To reduce these day-time measurements to the conditions assumed in calculating the profile we use (3.9), and find that the measured values shown should be raised by about $2' \cdot 7$, which, as will be seen, brings them into agreement with the calculated values. The Moon is shown rising at its southerly position at the major standstill. It will be seen how accurately the two limits of the perturbation are shown ($\Delta = 9' \cdot 0$).

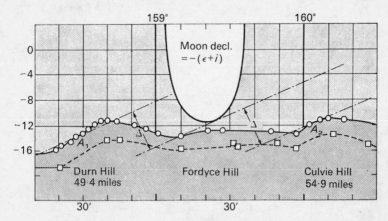

FIG. 9.2. From Mid Clyth, N 1/1. ○ = calculated, night-time, □ = measured, day-time.

The top outer row on the west side has an azimuth of about 24°. This is close to the azimuth of a small irregularity in a part of the horizon otherwise smooth and featureless. At the south end of this irregularity there is a deeper notch shown on the inset in Fig. 9.3. This figure also shows the stones that lie along the tops of the flat-topped ridge running east and west at the top of the rows. The spot levels show how the ground at the rows slopes up to the crest of this ridge, which is level to a foot or so. It evidently provided the observing platform for the Moon rising on the notch. We see on the ridge a fallen menhir 9 by $2\frac{1}{2}$ feet, traces of a cairn, and various boulders and stones, one of which, while small, is upright and orientated roughly on the notch. The 25-in O.S. shows a line of 5 or 6 stones running to the east, but most unfortunately the quarry has removed most of these. The approximate positions of these stones have been obtained by enlarging the Ordnance Survey to the scale of the figure.

The azimuth and altitude of the notch were carefully determined astronomically from three positions along the ridge. This enabled the effective distance of the notch to be found and made it possible to put on the plan arrows, as at Temple Wood, showing the stances from which the upper and lower limbs would emerge in the notch. In comparing this figure with Fig. 5.1

remember that in one case the Moon was rising and in the other setting. Both sites have a distant foresight in the south and both had a range of backsights for a notch in the north. In Temple Wood three or more of the backsights survive; perhaps there are three still at Mid Clyth: the fallen menhir, the north-west row in the sectors, and the small upright above the north-east

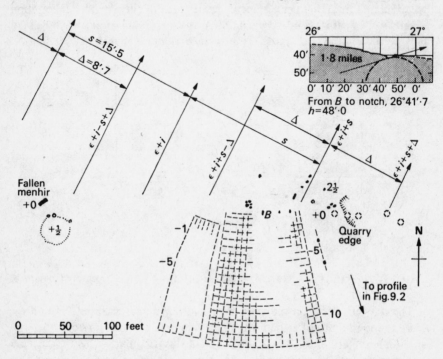

FIG. 9.3. Hill o' Many Stanes, Mid Clyth, N 1/1, ND 296384 (58° 19'·7, 3° 12'·3). Plan showing stances for various declinations.

corner. It may be noted that as one moves along the ridge to the west the notch becomes less distinct. This may explain the apparent attempt to raise the ground level near the menhir.

Perhaps it should be added that some 300 yards to the west on higher ground there is a somewhat irregular row of five or six boulders of various sizes. Including the very large stones at the west end, the row is 400 feet long and is orientated roughly about 33°. The notch from here is about 30°·6, $h = 0°·4$. This may be some form of early warning device, but it is not very convincing.

The spot levels show that the site of the rows slopes down to the south at 4 or 5°. The north side is steeper. Thus the centres from which the lines radiate are not visible from the greater part of the sectors, nor is the notch. This would have made it more difficult to set out the rows, but once they were in position it would not have been necessary to sight to the centre when using the grid.

From the bottom of the grid to the furthest centre is about 415 feet and to the mean centre of the main sector about 370 feet. These are smaller than the ideal calculated extrapolation length $4G$, but the error produced is almost negligible. It seems likely, however, that the builders had found out that the radii were on the short side. The first two lines of a modified structure, RR (Fig. 9.1) and the line next to it, had already been erected when the use of the site was discontinued.

Whether or not we accept the idea that the grid was a computer, the site is certainly a lunar observatory. The chance is remotely small that these stones are situated by accident at a spot which provides foresights for $\epsilon+i$ and $-(\epsilon+i)$ with perturbations, and provides them accurately. As has been pointed out, such a site is useless without a means of extrapolation.

9.3. Dirlot, ND 12264860, N 1/17

In the Caithness moors, two miles south from Westerdale and some 100 yards from the left bank of the Thurso River, there are remains of a score of small houses and a chapel. The cemetery is easily found, and the stone rows lie on an elevation some 400 yards to the west. The site can easily be missed because the remaining stones are mostly hidden in the undergrowth. Extensive prodding revealed 70–80, but one has to be careful, because below the vegetation and surface soil the ground is stony and hard, so that one can find an apparent stone almost anywhere. Only those showing, or definitely above the level of the hard ground, have been plotted on the survey in Fig. 9.4. Dryden shows roughly the same number of stones, but his survey is quite inadequate for our present purpose. Contours have been roughly surveyed and a glance at the figure shows that this site, like that at Mid Clyth, slopes up towards the narrow end of the sector. Beyond, as at Mid Clyth, the ground falls away steeply. The grid shown has been drawn with a base radius of 145 MY. Along this base the radial lines are spaced *exactly* 3 MY apart. It is evident that this scheme picks up the remains of the rows as well as can be expected in view of the inevitable displacement of stones by frost and general ground movement. Presumably the movement of the stones down the slope has been greater since it is difficult to trace any tendency for the stones to lie on regular arcs such as we find at Mid Clyth. The ground at the foot of the sector is nearly level and here there are four stones close to the bottom arc.

Dryden draws attention to traces of low mounds or 'cairns' on the flat summit. By analogy with Mid Clyth this summit has been assumed to be the observing platform. The mountain profile was measured carefully from here (Fig. 9.5). The altitudes are high enough to be free from the worst

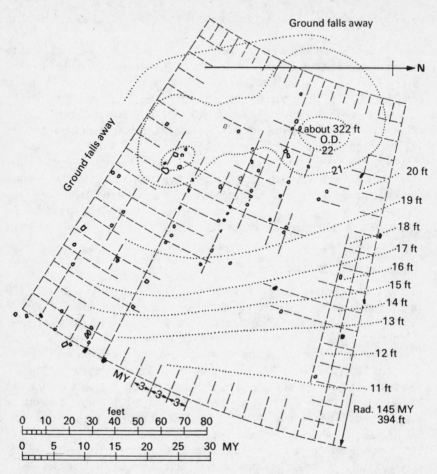

FIG. 9.4. Dirlot, N 1/17, ND 12264860 (58° 25′·0, 3° 30′·1). Contours at 1-ft intervals.

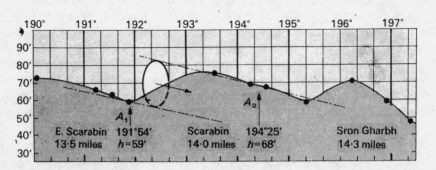

FIG. 9.5. Profile measured from the top of the rows at Dirlot, N 1/17. Moon setting with declination $= -(\epsilon + i) = -29° 2′·5$.

effects of refraction anomalies and so can be accepted as reasonably accurate ($\pm 0'\cdot 5$). The Moon is shown setting with declination $-(\epsilon+i) = -29° 2\frac{1}{2}'$. It is evident that here, as at Mid Clyth, the erectors succeeded in finding a site on a low eminence that gave the required declination in the south. But at Mid Clyth they were fortunate in finding a site on an eminence that also had a natural foresight for the Moon in the north. It is perhaps too much to believe that they would be able to repeat this at Dirlot, and in fact no natural foresight has so far been found. Failing a natural foresight the obvious thing to do was to erect an artificial foresight on a convenient ridge. It seems probable that they found a suitable ridge on the horizon at Achkeepster (16815197). The Ordnance Survey shows the 'site of' three standing stones near the road. Actually there is still one fallen menhir in the peat and two stones which may well have been upright. As seen from Dirlot the traffic on the road appears silhouetted on the horizon, but the foresight, 3·57 miles distant, would need to be larger than a single menhir to be clearly visible. Perhaps it was of timber or brushwood, renewed when the standstill approached. Or perhaps it was a cairn now built into the houses or into the road. The measured azimuth is 52°·3 and the altitude 0° 2', giving a declination of about $+19° 11'$, which is almost exactly $\epsilon-i+s+\Delta$ or the declination of the upper limb when the Moon was in its extreme northerly position at the *minor* standstill. Later it will be shown that the radius of the sector superimposed on the survey is within a few feet of that required theoretically to suit the distance to the Achkeepster foresight. In using the foresight it would never be necessary to move further south than the south mound, because from here the foresight shows the upper limb in its extreme position. There is room for movement to the north. If we are right is assuming that this foresight was really used then the Dirlot site was superior to, and supplemented, that at Mid Clyth, in that it could be used at both the major and the minor standstills.

In the field to the east of the graveyard there are three peculiar rows of low slabs set on edge as shown in Fig. 9.6. Many fences in Caithness are made of slabs and the rows at the graveyard may be the remains of a fence system. Against this the rows are not continuous and the stones are low and badly weathered, whereas it is said locally that slab fences fall down rather than weather down. A careful survey showed that no stone is more than a few inches off the mean line, which consequently can in each case be found to about ± 1 arc minute. It follows that we know the distance to the intersection of the outside lines is 7200 ± 100 feet. Perhaps it is a coincidence that this is so near the extrapolation length for the profile in Fig. 9.5, which is about $4G = 7320$ feet. The intersection point is on the other side of the river. This and the somewhat irregular nature of the ground make it difficult to believe that this peculiar method was used to store $4G$. If archaeologists ever show that these rows are really of Megalithic age there remains the problem of how they were used. As a guide to anyone who wishes to make further investigations, measurement of the mountain profile from the rows shows that the azimuths are about 55′ greater than those in Fig. 9.5. Near the village, and therefore between the graveyard and the main site, there are some stones said locally to be a stone circle, but if this was ever a circle the stones are now badly out of place.

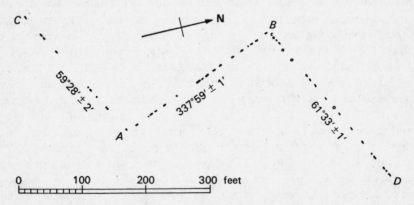

FIG. 9.6. Rows of slabs at Dirlot, N 1/17, ND 127487 (58° 25′·3, 3° 29′·7).

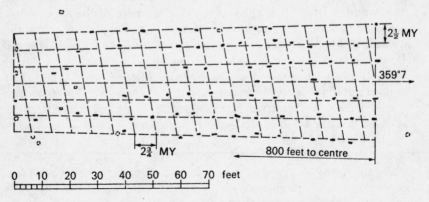

FIG. 9.7. Stone rows at Loch of Yarrows, N 1/7, ND 313440 (58° 22′·8, 3° 10′·5).

9.4. Loch of Yarrows, N 1/7, ND 313440

On the flat ground close to the north-east corner of the Loch of Yarrows, some 5 miles south from Wick, there are still at least sixty-six small stones in position, but the early Ordnance Survey shows more stones extending to the north. Cultivation of the field has almost certainly reduced the width as well as the length. Fig. 9.7 shows a reproduction of a carefully made large-scale plan. This site is on boulder clay so the slightest inclination of the surface can, over the centuries, produce irregular movement. Nevertheless, the grid shown seems to fit reasonably well. The inclined cross lines are interesting. This scheme would of course work just as well as the circular arcs at Mid Clyth.

From the slightly higher ground, where the Ordnance Survey shows the last stone to the north, at an azimuth of about 191°·0, there is on the Ordnance Survey a cairn. This line gives a declination close to $-(\epsilon+i-\Delta-s)$ and an extrapolation length $4G$ of about 760 feet, which is of the same order as the radius of the rows. Perhaps it should be said that there is an interesting alternative possibility. On the hilltop 1100 yards to the south-south-east there are two large menhirs, the line joining them being about 342°. Some 400 feet to the east of these on a flat piece of ground 40 feet lower there are four or five stones, some of which look very like fallen menhirs. The orientation of the two upper menhirs draws attention to the slope down from Tannach Hill to the left. In this slope there is an almost imperceptible break. This spot was examined and showed a peat covering with the hard bottom showing just at the break. Before the peat grew the break might have been more evident. A flag was placed at the spot and viewed from near the fallen menhirs; this showed a declination of $\epsilon+i$ with $4G = 765$ feet. Looking from the flag, the two tall menhirs stand out clearly and show a declination of about $-(\epsilon+i-s-\Delta)$ and the same $4G$. So the rows beside the loch could have been placed at a spot convenient to both backsights. This is of course pure speculation and, on the whole, the first suggestion given above seems the more likely. A more detailed examination might settle the matter. Perhaps the rows served three purposes.

9.5. Camster, N 1/14, ND 260438

The Grey Cairns of Camster are well known and well worth a visit. Some 140 yards south from the smaller is a small burial cairn and 120 yards south from this are the stone rows. Dryden's survey shows thirty-three stones, but after an hour's prodding three of us had found only 14 definite stones and a dozen or so suspected buried stones. The survey in Fig. 9.8 shows that it is not possible to be perfectly certain of the radius of the sector. That drawn has a radius of 200 MY or 544 feet. It seems, however, that the spacing along the base has been exactly $1\frac{1}{2}$ MY and this interval has also been used radially with reasonable success. As in the other known inclined cases the narrow end of the sector lies uphill from the wider base.

The site is in a valley, which narrows as it rises to the south. As a result the Moon, in its southern extreme position at a major standstill, would show for a short time only as it crossed the gap at the top of the valley. Where the hill rises smoothly and gently from the west side of the valley a boulder is seen on the horizon. Measured from the cairn near the rows this gives an azimuth of 193° 30′ and an altitude of 1° 24′. The corresponding declination is $-28°\,40'$ or about $-(\epsilon+i-s-\Delta)$. It follows that the boulder, or an artificial foresight at it, would give lunar standstill declinations from positions just above the rows. The calculated value of the extrapolation length is $4G = 606$ feet, against the 544 feet used to draw the grid. So here again we have a sector of the radius necessary to suit the foresight.

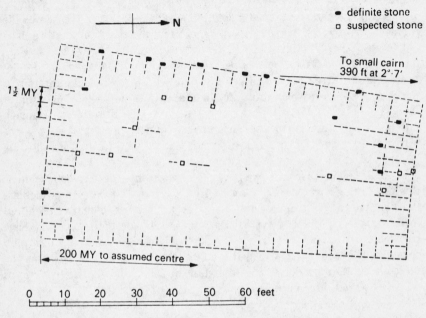

FIG. 9.8. Stone rows at Camster, N 1/14, ND 260438 (58° 52′·6, 3° 15′·9).

It would seem that excavation is necessary to decide definitely (1) what the radius really was, and (2) if the sector extended further to the east or west.

9.6. Using the sectors

As we have seen, there are two geometrical methods of finding the extrapolation distance, by the use of a triangle, Fig. 8.3, or by the use of a sector, Fig. 8.4. We do not expect to find any trace of the triangle method. All that was necessary was a knowledge of the length G and $4G$. Looking at Fig. 9.9 we see why the triangle construction could not be left permanently set out in stone on the ground. All the work would be done between A and F, but here the stone rows would get so close that confusion would be inevitable unless very small, and therefore impermanent, stones were used. Provided two people were available, one would sight from the line BC to A and the other would place rods as directed. On the other hand, the sector can be permanent and can be operated by one man (Fig. 9.10).

For either method a knowledge of the lengths G and $4G$ is essential, not only for setting out the site but for using it. The length G might have been known as a length in yards or it might have been stored as a readily measurable length on the ground.

How then was G obtained? It might have been found by a long trial-and-error process, but a simple direct method was available with plenty of opportunity to practise it. At any standstill there are twenty or more lunations

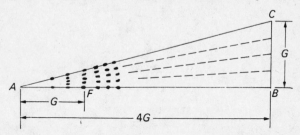

FIG. 9.9. Showing that stone rows cannot be used with the triangle method.

for which the stake positions will fall near a site arranged for the maximum. While only one of these can provide the maximum many of them provide an opportunity to measure G. In Fig. 9.11 three nights' observation have provided the positions M, T, and W. Then the distance from T to the point midway between M and W is $4G$, and so G is found.

An ability to make use of this method demands the kind of knowledge we should expect these people to have had. They had certainly been studying stake positions for years at dozens of observatories and they would certainly have tried to relate the stake positions found in the three-stake case in Fig. 9.11 with the two-stake case.

Consider the setting out of Avebury (Thom 1967, frontispiece). An analysis of this ring (op. cit., p. 90) shows that its development must have taken years of trial and error. It would be set out again and again. The south-west arc has a radius of 750 MY and could not have been set out by a rope from the centre, which lies far outside the ditch and bank. The elasticity of a rope of this length would alone have prohibited its use and the other difficulties are obvious. Today one might calculate the offsets from the chord. In Megalithic times the corresponding method would have been to set out by measuring rods (from the centre) the ends and the middle of the arc. Then the sagitta for the whole arc could be measured. One-quarter of this is the sagitta for the half-arcs just as in Fig. 9.11. The quarter-arcs follow and so on as often as is necessary. Any method that can be suggested for setting out the Avebury arcs (even the shorter arcs) with the accuracy that we find there demands a knowledge of the geometry of flat arcs.

Whatever method was used, they did find G at Mid Clyth and elsewhere. Knowing G they could deal with those lunations where the distance between two successive stake positions happened to be small. They would find the mid-position and then advance a distance G from there. Incidentally, this also gave them p, which perhaps explains why the grids are prepared to use p and not $2p$; or was this simply to economize space? But p might be anything from zero to $2G$, and when they tried to apply the same method when p was large they would find it was badly in error. In fact in the limiting case when $p = 2G$ the total movement is $2G$ and not G (Fig. 9.12). But since it

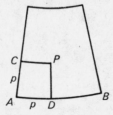

FIG. 9.10. Use of grid for finding $\eta = AD - CP$.

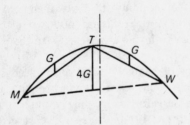

FIG. 9.11. Measuring G from 3 days' stake positions.

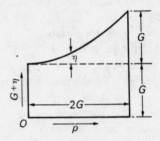

FIG. 9.12. Total correction to mid-point.

was nearly correct to use G for a range of small values the relation could not be linear. How they would have pictured the position we do not know. They were faced with a quadratic relationship. The true correction is parabolic, as shown in Fig. 9.12. For small values of p the total correction stays close to G, but it then rises more and more steeply to reach $2G$ when p is $2G$. This follows from Chapter 8, where the true value is shown to be

$$G + p^2/4G, \text{ or, as we have written it, } G + \eta.$$

The step that resulted in the geometrical equivalent to this expression must be regarded as one of man's great achievements. Today it is easy to get the result algebraically. These people certainly had no such aid.

Earlier in this chapter will be found four examples where the sectors set out on the ground show that they had been used in conjunction with a lunar site. In all four the radius of the sector is approximately equal to the length

$4G$ that we find theoretically. At Mid Clyth the base and height of the main sector is G, which, as has been shown, is the largest value needed, but the radius is on the small side. The error thereby produced in the final stake position is negligibly small unless p happens to be near its limiting value G, and even then it would not be serious. If, as has already been suggested, the sector was in the process of modification to increase its radius, the error would have been reduced. Their method of finding the correct radius may have been one of trial and error. We cannot yet be certain that they realized that the correct value was $4G$. It is possible that at the end they had got this far. In this connection one would like to know the relative dates of the sites; e.g. was Temple Wood later than Mid Clyth?

9.7. Let us now consider the possibility that when p was greater than G they did not use the above method, but preferred to find y_L, the necessary movement from the most advanced of the two observed positions. Examine Fig. 8.2 and note that when L is at M, y_R is $4G$ and p is $2G$. Provided p is nearly $2G$, i.e. provided L is near M, y_L remains small, but when p is zero y_L is G.

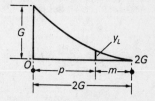

FIG. 9.13. Total correction y_L to position of advanced stake L.

This is shown in Fig. 9.13. We have here the same parabola as in Fig. 9.11, but it is reversed. It follows that if we write $m = 2G-p$ we get, as in (8.11),

$$y_L = m^2/4G.$$

Hence when p lies between 0 and G we can use $\eta = p^2/4G$,   (9.1)

and when p lies between G and $2G$ we can use $y_L = m^2/4G$.   (9.2)

The evidence that both of these were in use is that the main sector at Mid Clyth does not make provision for values of p (or of m) greater than G. In fact on half of the occasions when the computing grid was wanted it would fail to supply a direct answer unless both (9.1) and (9.2) were in use. At Dirlot G is 100 feet and so the base width of 147 feet provides an overlap between the two methods, but is insufficient to operate on one of the methods all the time.

9.8. The extrapolation lengths

The information regarding these lengths, as given by the four sites with sectors, is collected in Table 9.1. This allows a direct comparison to be made between the theoretical lengths, calculated from the distance to the foresight, and the radii of the sectors. The second part of the table has been included to show that at some other important sites there may still be a record of G or $4G$.

Table 9.1. *Comparison of observed and theoretical extrapolation lengths G or 4G*

	Site	Decl.	$dA/d\delta$	D (miles)	θ	G (feet)	$4G$ (feet)	L = length on site	Remarks
Sites with sectors	Mid Clyth	$(\epsilon+i)$ R	3·70	1·80	90°		503	360	Radius of main sector
	Mid Clyth	$(\epsilon+i)$ R	3·70	1·80	90°		503	413	Radius of south-west sector
	Mid Clyth	$(\epsilon+i)$ R	3·70	1·80	90°	126		132	Base of main sector
	Dirlot	$(\epsilon-i)$ R	2·29	3·57	90°		398	394	Radius of sector
	Dirlot	$(\epsilon-i)$ R	2·29	3·57	90°	100		147	Base of sector
	L. of Yarrows	$(\epsilon+i)$ S	8·90	1·14	90°		756	800	Radius of rows
	L. of Yarrows	$(\epsilon+i)$ S	4·10	2·45	90°		765	800	Radius of rows
	L. of Yarrows	$-(\epsilon+i)$ R	4·46	2·45	90°		826	800	Radius of rows
	Camster	$-(\epsilon+i)$ S	7·17	1·12	90°		606	544	Radius of sector
Sites with G or $4G$ on the ground	Temple Wood	$+(\epsilon+i)$ S	2·30	1·25	67°		236	260	Hard patch to S_1 (see text)
	Temple Wood	$-(\epsilon+i)$ S	3·36	3·97	90°		1010	983	Circle to S_1
	Fowlis Wester	$+(\epsilon+i)$ R	3·08	7·30	90°	422		452	E to N
	Fowlis Wester	$+(\epsilon+i)$ S	2·48	1·06	90°	49		53	E to L
								43	E to M
	Stillaig	$+(\epsilon+i)$ S	2·8	13·6	90°	720	2880	2200	Between the two menhirs
	Glen Prosen	$+(\epsilon+i)$ S	5·2	0·43	90°	42	168	113	Length of alignment (today)
	Kell Burn	$-(\epsilon-i)$ R	2·2	2·4	90°	64	256	310	Length of alignment (today)

$$G = 18\cdot9 \times D \times dA/d\delta \text{ for } \epsilon+i$$
$$= 12\cdot2 \times D \times dA/d\delta \text{ for } \epsilon-i$$

R = rising Moon. S = setting Moon. D = distance to foresight. θ = angle assumed between foresight and observer's line of movement.

What kind of accuracy was necessary in the determination of the two lengths G and $4G$? We have for the movement from the position midway between the stakes $G+\eta$, and for the movement from the most advanced stake y_L, where $\eta = p^2/4G$ and $y_L = m^2/4G$. Since either method may be used to give the position for the maximum declination at that lunation we have seen that

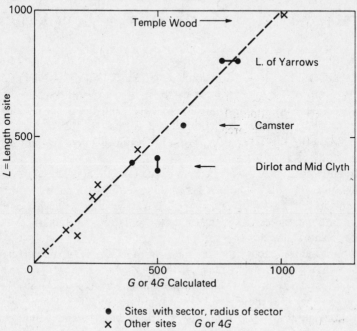

FIG. 9.14. Extrapolation lengths.

neither p nor m need ever be greater than G. Hence neither η nor y_L need ever be greater than $G/4$. Since G corresponds to 12′ of declination, an η of amount $G/4$ corresponds to 3′. Hence, when using the $G+\eta$ method, to avoid an error greater than 1′ in declination G should be known to 1 part in 12 or 8 per cent, and η to 1 part in 3 or 33 per cent. Since an error of 1 per cent in η (or y_L) is produced by 1 per cent in $4G$, the latter need only be known to 33 per cent. Bear in mind that until we have proved that the erectors knew that the correct radius for the sectors was $4G$ we must treat the quantities G and $4G$ as independent entities.

In Fig. 9.14 the lengths of the radii found on the ground are plotted against the theoretical value $4G$. It is to be noted that p or m would in general be much smaller than their maximum values. Hence a slightly erroneous value of the radius would usually have very little effect. It thus appears that the values used were of sufficient accuracy.

10

THE WORK AT THE OBSERVATORIES

10.1. In this chapter the methods probably used at the more complete observatories will be described in some detail, but it will be assumed that the reader is aware of the necessity for extrapolation and understands broadly how it might have been done. It will be assumed that the observatories were built primarily for eclipse prediction, but it is possible that the Megalithic scientist was using this as an excuse to 'obtain funds' to enable him to make a deeper study of astronomy.

For predicting any event a calendar is necessary. These people made use of a highly developed calendar (Thom 1965, 1967), which was controlled by the Sun just as ours is today. It was necessary to have at least one good calendar line associated with any lunar observatory, and there is enough evidence to show that this was so.

The object then was to predict the dates of the maxima of the perturbation cycle. We know today that for this two things had to be found: (1) the period 173·3 days, and (2) the date of one maximum. Today we know that the period is constant. But these people had to find this out. The constancy would be obscured initially by the difficulty described in § 2.8 and would become apparent only when tested by observation of the node at an observatory like Temple Wood. If this observatory were used for, say, 20 years the period would be known accurately. It is probable that controversy regarding this and other matters went on for generations, and this perhaps explains why there are numerous observatories throughout the country. Protagonists of opposing theories might have had their own observatory or even group of observatories.

But at any observatory operated for several standstills the observers must have found inexplicable anomalies. I refer to the changes that would be observed to take place due to the fact that the effective parallax at the standstills varied with a long period (§ 7.5). There were two possible ways of overcoming this difficulty. In theory it is possible to find the date of the maximum of the perturbation cycle from observations made at three successive declination maxima near the date of the perturbation maximum. Alternatively it could be obtained by interpolating from the date of two nodes (for example N and M, Fig. 2.3), one on each side of a maximum or a minimum. If one node had been made early by parallax the other would have been late. So the time midway between would have been the time of the maximum or the time of the minimum. This was probably the use of the group Q at Temple Wood.

10.2. It was desirable, if not in fact necessary, to know the date of the standstill in advance, and there was a convenient method available. In Fig. 2.2 we see the declination limits throughout the 18-year cycle. The node of the upper curve is at B, and at B the declination is equal to ϵ, the obliquity of the ecliptic. At first sight it appears that all we have to do is to watch for the lunation when the Moon in its most northerly position sets on the marks established for the Sun at the summer solstice. Then 18·6/4, i.e. 4·65, years later is the standstill. But when the Moon is seen on the Sun's foresight it has not got the Sun's declination. This is because the Moon is so much nearer to us than the Sun that its parallax is much greater. A short calculation shows that in these latitudes this effect alters the interval to the standstill by about half a year, and that this interval may be affected by as much as 30 days by the state of the perturbation when the Moon is on the solstitial foresight.

The reader will have noticed that the effect of parallax on the time when the Moon is on the marks for the winter solstice is of opposite sign. The manner in which the two could have been combined to give better accuracy is obvious. We do not know which method was favoured, but the fact that we find solstitial foresights near (and sometimes at) lunar observatories suggests that they were so used. They would have provided an ideal method for determining the 18·6-year *period*.

The explanations hitherto given about how the observatories may have been worked will now be illustrated and augmented by an imaginary dialogue between an instructor and a novice at Temple Wood. Extrapolation has already been so fully covered that it will not be included. The reader is advised to refer to Fig. 5.1.

10.3. Dialogue

Instructor. Go to Kintraw at the time I tell you and watch for the lunation when the Moon at its furthest south vanishes behind Beinn Shiantaidh and then shows briefly before going under Beinn à Chaolais. The main standstill will take place about 5 years and 50 days later. Temple Wood is better equipped to observe this standstill than any other observatory, even the famous observatories in Caithness. Shortly before the standstill you will begin to observe to Bellanoch Hill in the South. You will then be ready 14 days later for the setting in the notch, which you see above and behind the circle with the little box socket.

I shall now describe in detail how to observe to the notch, but you must also make a similar set of observations to Bellanoch Hill. The only difference is that at the Hill there are two foresights, one for the upper and one for the lower limb, so that dual backsights are not necessary. Remember that the distance that I call G is 20 yards for the notch and 90 for Bellanoch Hill. The stones showing these distances are small at Temple Wood and may be lost or moved. We have set the main backsights well in the ground so that they are unlikely to be disturbed.

While you are observing the upper limb in the notch your companion will observe the lower. If you use hazel rods and your companion ash, there should be no confusion, even at night. At every lunation your object is to establish by extrapolation a point on the ground, and this point you will mark by a *large* hazel stake marked with the date. When the time comes near you will carry a *small* stake and, moving on the line of the stones S_2 S_1 S_5, but always remaining upright, you will get into such a position that the upper limb just twinkles and no more as it passes through the notch. If the position you find is within 100 yards of the stones you will place there the first small stake. If you are very lucky and find exactly the same position next night then measure G to the left and place there the large hazel stake for the lunation. Another easy case is when the distance between two successive twinkling positions is nearly $4G$, because then the most advanced stake, that on the left, shows where to place the large stake.

Novice. What do I do if the distance between the two most advanced stakes is neither zero nor $4G$?

Instructor. You should move to the left from the most advanced stake a distance (m) that you will find by a geometrical method that I shall teach you, and you should place the large stake there.

Novice. I think you once told me there was another method.

Instructor. Yes, the Caithness people have a method of which they are very proud. They say it is very accurate.

Novice. Do they always use it?

Instructor. No. They use it when the distance between successive stakes is small. When the distance is larger they employ a method that is very like ours. Both methods use in the extrapolation construction a length that is not very different from $4G$. Indeed it is thought by some that it should be exactly $4G$. For Bellanoch Hill it is the distance from the main circle to S_1, and for the notch it is from the cairn to S_1.

By the method I have just explained you should establish a large stake for each lunation. For the upper limb the stone marking the node of the wobble is S_4. When you find you have two successive large hazel stakes, one on one side of S_4 and one on the other, you will divide the distance between them into twenty-seven equal parts, or as many parts as there were days in the lunation. Suppose that the stone S_4 is at the sixth division from the second stake. Then you have found the date of the node, because it occurred six days earlier than the date on which you placed the second large stake. If the Moon has been getting further north at each lunation you will wait until it is coming south about 80 days later and again you will establish two large stakes one on each side of the node. The date you thereby find for this second passage through the node may be about half a period, i.e. 86 days, later than the first, but we find this interval changes slowly from standstill to standstill. The date midway between the two passages will be the date on which the Moon came furthest north, and you may have seen the eclipse or eclipses that took place at the full or new Moon nearest to that date.

Meanwhile your companion is establishing stakes of ash for the lower limb. His stakes will be about 65 yards to the right of yours. To use the group Q you should place each night a large stake of *oak* midway between your stake and that of your companion. You will understand that the oak stakes are not for either limb but for the centre of the Moon's disc. Since the group Q has been placed to show the node for the Moon's centre you should use the oak stakes with Q just as I have described for the hazel stakes with S_4.

Novice. I understand you to say that I must always place most reliance on the result obtained by taking the time midway between the times of the two nodes nearest to the standstill. How can I be sure that I have used the nodes nearest to the standstill?

Instructor. By watching the positions of the large stakes at the intermediate maximum or minimum.

Novice. Can I not use these stakes to find directly when the wobble was at its maximum?

Instructor. Yes, but the day on which the extreme large stake (D, Fig. 2.3), i.e. the one furthest to the left, was placed is not necessarily the date of the maximum. There may be a small correction, which you can find like this. Measure the distance between the stakes for the preceding and following lunations (C and E). If you are using the notch the correction is roughly 1 day for every yard in this distance. For Bellanoch Hill it is about 1 day for every 4 yards.

Novice. What do I do if I find that the Bellanoch Hill observations are giving a different date?

Instructor. You should take an average. But we think that the notch is more reliable, because the sight line to Bellanoch Hill is lower and so is more likely to be affected by those vapours on the horizon that we know can upset our observations.

Novice. If clouds or mist or a new Moon prevent observations to both Bellanoch Hill and the notch, can I do anything?

Instructor. This is most unlikely. You will normally make at least four independent determinations on each foresight of the date you want. There will be one from the node and three from those maxima or minima that occur within half a year of the standstill. But if you miss a whole standstill it will be 9 years before you get another opportunity, at the minor standstill at Kintraw. The ground there is so restricted that accurate work is almost impossible, and we regard lunar work done there as more in the nature of a check. Perhaps you could get permission to use the observatory high up on Ben Turc in Kintyre. It has foresights for both standstills, and they can sometimes observe when we are in mist. The drawback is that the ground is not so level as at Temple Wood, and extrapolation is more difficult.

Novice. And when I have found the date of the maximum how do I find the eclipse times?

Instructor. You should add multiples of 173 days to the date you have found and all these dates will be in the middle of the danger periods. If a full Moon happens within 14 days of one of these dates it will be eclipsed and if a new Moon happens it will probably eclipse the Sun. Continue to add intervals of 173 days till you get another opportunity to observe. I hear that some observatories now add 174 days every third or fourth period, but do not know if they really have enough evidence for this.

Novice. If I lose my calendar reckoning can I pick it up again?

Instructor. Yes, there is a calendar foresight at Kintraw, but if you must do it yourself you had better get the men in Knapdale to show you the stone at Kilberry, which is very reliable in showing the equinox.

10.4. The observers' ideas

The workers at the observatories must have attempted to explain what they observed. We may speculate as to what their ideas were. Assuming freedom from dogma, they might have come near the truth regarding the shape of the Earth and Moon. The Sun illuminating the edge of the new Moon must have suggested to these keen-eyed observers that the Moon was spherical. They would have seen how the full Moon was opposite the Sun.

The shadow of an observer's head as seen by him retains its shape whether it falls on a flat surface or on a boulder, and so, if someone once thought of the world being round, its shadow on the Moon would provide confirmation. Once the idea was implanted there were other confirmatory clues. There are standing stones in Shetland, and from the hilltops in Unst, the furthest north of the Shetlands, the Moon in its most northerly position at the standstills *did not set.* The upper limb was in fact circumpolar. In its most southerly position the Moon would barely rise above even a low horizon. These phenomena must have been very striking to an observer trained, for example, in the south of England. Another clue is the manner in which an island is seen to sink below the sea horizon by a voyager as his distance from it increases, and the way in which he can bring it back into view by climbing a hill.

Reasoning without the evidence of the Shetland circumpolar Moon the Greeks deduced that the Earth was a sphere, and the ancient Britons may have arrived at the same conclusion.

How much further could their more advanced thinkers have gone? Two observers using the upper and lower limb as described previously would have been aware of the variation in the apparent diameter of the Moon on the northern foresight. They would probably have noticed how an increase in diameter was connected with the decreased declination brought about by parallax. This kind of thing would have been forced on their attention during the long series of observations that must have preceded the erection of observatories like Temple Wood and Mid Clyth. How they would have interpreted their measurements we do not know, but what we do know is that their observing technique was sufficiently accurate to provide data that might have revealed much if properly interpreted.

11

CONCLUSIONS

IT has been shown elsewhere that there existed in Britain in Megalithic times a widespread knowledge of geometry. We find designs drawn with the same conventions set out on the ground and inscribed on rocks and stones. In both there is the same insistence on integral lengths. The linear unit that we find on the rock designs is 0·816 inch or exactly one-fortieth of the Megalithic yard used in ground plans. The designer undoubtedly used a set of beam compasses with the distance between the inscribing points advancing by units or half units. This explains the preoccupation with integral lengths and the necessity of using triangles with sides of integral length satisfying the Pythagorean theorem.

With this background we need not be surprised to find an intense interest in astronomy. Time of night was found by the stars rising, transiting, or setting. Time of year came from a highly developed calendar, linked accurately to the Sun in such a manner that the necessity for inserting the intercalary day every fourth year would have become apparent in a few years. I have shown elsewhere (Thom 1967) that the calendar itself was capable of giving the exact day of the solstice, and yet we find accurate solstitial observatories. In Chapter 10 it is suggested that these were used to predict the date of the coming standstill, but this use did not need the accuracy that we find at, for example, Kintraw. At Kintraw a 5 °F change in temperature would affect the Sun's apparent declination by about 0'·5 and so would have been obvious. Here then at Kintraw is an instrument capable of showing clearly that on a particularly cold midwinter evening the Sun appeared slightly raised.

It was only natural that a people looking critically at the setting Sun would use the same observing method on the Moon. But here they found a much more complicated motion. They would see that it was only at the standstills that anything like repeatable results could be obtained. But the rapidity with which the Moon passes through the monthly declination maximum set them a serious problem, namely that of extrapolation. Did they solve this problem by first making it geometrical? If they tried the effect of stepping back each night as shown in Fig. 1.1 they would have been able to apply their knowledge of the geometry of the flat arc. We know how much time they must have spent on the problem at numerous observatories throughout the country, and it would be strange indeed if they had not somewhere tried out this method of avoiding confusion as the stake position moved first one way and then the other. This method would show the constancy of what we have called the sagitta (G), and would have led to the method of finding G at any site with sufficient clear ground (§ 9.6).

They were now ready to tackle the problem of the quadratic relation between the stake interval and the extrapolation distance. The evidence suggests strongly that they solved the problem in an entirely satisfactory manner, perhaps even more satisfactory than the inevitable anomalies in the apparent motion allowed them to realize. They could now place the stake for the monthly declination maximum. If we have formed a correct idea of their method of thought then the next step was obvious. They would have applied the same type of reasoning to the monthly maxima as they had used in handling the nightly stake positions at the declination maxima. This gave them, as we have seen, two methods of finding in retrospect the exact date of the perturbation maximum. They were also in a position to demonstrate the constancy of the 173·3-day period and to apply it successively to predict the dates of the maxima until the next opportunity of observing, i.e. at the next standstill.

While the existence of the lunar observatories is beyond dispute, there seems to be no definite evidence that the main object was eclipse prediction; and if it were, why are there so many observatories? Possible answers are (1) poor communications, (2) lack of uniformity in the calendars used in different districts, (3) replacement of obsolete observatories by more up-to-date ones. Of the three, the last seems to be the most likely. To settle this point conclusively we need some independent method of dating by archaeological methods. The co-operation of archaeologists is also needed to find out if any of the sites were re-erected. Assuming that the cult lasted for several centuries the obliquity changes would make it desirable to move the backsights. Can this be proved or disproved by excavation or are present excavation techniques or interpretations of excavations still too crude? Large menhirs go deep into the ground, and some trace of a change in position should surely be left. In some places we want to know if there are traces of menhirs now removed, and in others, e.g. Mid Clyth, we want to know the original position of fallen menhirs.

The intense interest taken in the Moon's movements must have led the more acute minds to seek a deeper understanding. These people were certainly not inferior to us in ability to think. How much did scientific curiosity affect the work at the observatories and how much could the observatories have contributed to knowledge?

The fluctuating nature of the lengths of the Synodic and tropical months must have been puzzling, and the constancy of the 173·3-day period would have been some relief. If they had noticed at the solstitial sites the effect of the progressive fall in the value of the obliquity they would be prepared for a similar effect on the Moon. But on a short run of observations this is obscured by the peculiar effect of parallax described in § 7.5. A long series of observations extending over several centuries could have shown the periodic nature of this apparent parallax fluctuation; it has a double amplitude of about 7′. If they had not detected this it must have been by chance that the lunar observatories were erected from observations extending through exactly the right period of time to show so nearly the same value of ϵ as we find at the solstitial observatories.

The erectors evidently attached great importance to lunar sites. This is apparent from the complexity of the sites in Caithness and the large menhirs and alignments used elsewhere. The list of known sites includes nearly a dozen alignments, and among these are to be found some of the most impressive alignments in Britain, e.g. Callanish, Ballymeanach, Escart, and Parc-y-Meirw. An outstanding feature is the height of many of the menhirs, e.g. Knockstaple 11 feet, Parc-y-Meirw 11 feet, Campbelltown 11 feet, Camus an Stacca 12 feet, Balemartin 12 feet, Lundin Links 14 feet, Callanish 14 feet, and Beacharr 15 feet. Other sites may contain more massive stones, but the lunar sites often have the tallest menhirs. The alignments indicated the foresight and, when there is (now) only a single menhir, if it was a slab the flat faces were orientated on the foresight.

Judging by those districts that have been closely examined, it is probably safe to say that at least one lunar site was to be found in each part of the country where there are other Megalithic remains. On the west coast of Scotland we find them in Lewis, North Uist, Mull, Tiree, Jura, Gigha, Kintyre, and other parts of Argyllshire. We cannot speak about Skye, because the Church caused nearly all the stones in the island to be thrown down, just as in earlier years papal authority was given for the destruction of Avebury (Keiller 1965).

As is to be expected, we find the same general distribution of calendar sites. In this connection it should be remembered that one calendar line in a district is sufficient to keep the calendar linked to the Sun.

There are solstitial sites in many places, but only in south Argyllshire do we find a group with foresights of sufficient accuracy to permit of the kind of analysis attempted in Chapter 4. South Argyllshire is also peculiarly rich in lunar sites. In the district covered by the map in Fig. 11.1 there are over a dozen known sites, and the examination of Islay and Arran is incomplete. The reason for this large number is not clear, but one may wonder if some of these stones belong to the earlier days of the cult when it was considered that the backsight ought to be set up for the limit or limits of the perturbation rather than for its node. It will be noticed that apart from the fully developed observatories there is only one stone (Campbelltown) for the node. Are we seeing in the duplication of observatories an attempt to minimize the effects of cloudy or misty weather, or did poor communications

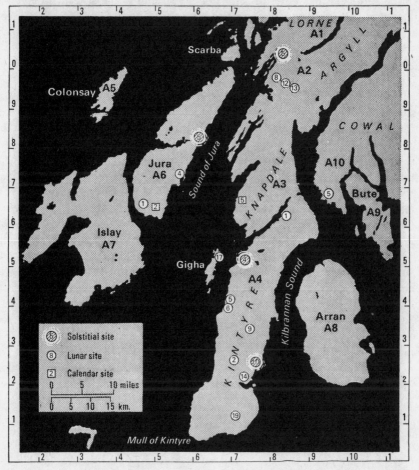

FIG. 11.1. Lunar, solar, and calendar sites in south Argyllshire.

make it desirable for each district to be independent? Neither explanation seems entirely satisfactory.

Anyone who makes a detailed study of the more advanced sites like Temple Wood and Ballymeanach will realize that the people who built them possessed a highly developed knowledge of the complicated movements of the Moon in the sky, and that they must have employed some form of extrapolation. The implications are far-reaching. The design of the necessary sectors, whether obtained by pure reason or by some complex empirical operation, demanded a highly trained intellect. The discipline necessary could not have arisen out of nothing. There must have been behind it a school or a system of mathematical reasoning, also evidenced by the remarkable designs that we find in the complex rings described in Thom 1967, and in the so-called cup-and-ring marks. A study of the latter will be found in Thom 1968, 1969. They seem to show a concentration on trial and error, which may have been applied successfully to the extrapolation problem. Nevertheless, the trials, to be ultimately successful, must have been guided by rather more than a mathematical intuition. How far advanced they really were is not yet clear.

It is to be hoped that this monograph does not give the impression that a study of these remains from the astronomical point of view is complete. It is only begun. But it must be pursued quickly before the sites suffer further damage. In this century, to the author's knowledge, aerodromes, roads, reservoirs, housing, quarries, agriculture, and forestry have all taken their toll, and the pace of destruction is quickening. One well-meaning individual took a stone into his garden 'to preserve it'. Another menhir was cut up by a mason to make lintels; farmers have removed large outliers; and so it goes on. The author makes a plea for the position of every stone near a site, however insignificant-looking, to be recorded exactly, before the information it may hold is lost for ever. Even at this late day something may be saved. Archaeologists and archaeological societies are aware of the danger, as is also the Forestry Commission, but we need the co-operation of the man in the street. The archaeological remains in which this country is so rich are our heritage and our responsibility. We must do our best to preserve them for posterity.

APPENDIX A

Some astronomical definitions

THE reader is referred to any good textbook on spherical astronomy, but the following notes may be useful for reference.

A *great circle* on a sphere is a circle made by a plane passing through the centre of the sphere. Any circle made by a plane cutting the sphere but not passing through the centre is known as a *small circle*.

The *pole* of a great circle is the point where a line normal to the plane of the great circle at its centre cuts the sphere, e.g. the zenith is the pole of the horizon.

The *celestial equator*, or more simply the *equator*, is the great circle in which the plane of the Earth's equator cuts the celestial sphere.

The *meridian* is the great circle on the celestial sphere that passes through the observer's zenith and the pole of the celestial equator.

The *hour angle* of a celestial body is the angle between the observer's meridian and a meridian that would contain the body. It is a measure of the time that has elapsed since the body was on the observer's meridian.

Right ascension and *declination* on the celestial sphere correspond to longitude and latitude on the Earth. Whereas longitude is measured from the Greenwich meridian, right ascension has its zero at the First Point of Aries, which is the position of the Sun at the Vernal Equinox, or simply the equinox. The declination of a star can be thought of as the latitude of a point on the Earth immediately under the star. In other words, it is the latitude of an observer who once a night finds the star passing through his zenith. Positive and negative declinations refer to stars north and south of the equator.

Table A.1. *Length of the year and of the lunar months in days*

Year or month	Definition	Length in A.D. 1900 (days)	Length in 1700 B.C. (days)
Tropical year	Equinox to equinox	365·24220	365·24242
Eclipse year	Node to node	346·62003	346·61888
Synodical month	New Moon to new Moon	29·53059	29·53060
Sidereal month	Fixed star to fixed star	27·32166	27·32167
Tropical month	Equinox to equinox	27·32158	27·32159
Draconic month	Node to node	27·21222	27·21222
Anomalistic month	Perigee to perigee	27·55455	27·55460

The *azimuth* of a body, celestial or terrestrial, is the direction in which we have to look to see it, or, more formally, it is the angle between the plane of the meridian and the great circle passing through the zenith and the body.

The *altitude* of a body is the angle of elevation to the body from the horizontal plane. It is measured along the vertical circle defining the azimuth. The difference between apparent and true altitude is dealt with in Chapter 3.

The time taken by the Sun to make one revolution relative to the equinox is called the *tropical year*, and the time relative to the nodes of the Moon's orbit the *eclipse year*. There are five different kinds of lunar 'month', which must not be confused. Each of these is the mean interval of time taken by the Moon to make one revolution relative to a point defined in Table A.1.

Individual values of the various lunar months may be different by a day or two from the values given, but the means remain sensibly constant, as can be seen by the very small changes shown in 3600 years. From the first two lines of the table it follows that the nodes of the lunar orbit rotate relative to the equinox in 18·6133 years (A.D. 1900). In 1700 B.C. the period was 18·6119 years.

Confusion may arise if the reader does not understand that in § 2.2 the word *node* refers to the Moon's orbit whereas in § 5.5 and § 10.3 it refers to the mid-point of the perturbation oscillation.

APPENDIX B

Surveying a site

B.1. The theodolite

I T is assumed that the reader is familiar with the construction, adjustment, and use of the theodolite. The notes that follow are intended to stress those points that are important in surveying a site and more particularly in measuring up a profile.

Textbooks usually deal separately with making a survey and with determining azimuth. But for our present purpose the determination of azimuth using the Sun has to be done so often that the serious worker must make himself so familiar with the process that it becomes automatic. Consider a common example where we have determined azimuth at one station and wish to transfer to a second station perhaps less than 100 feet away. Instead of trying to do this by the time-consuming method of accurate centring and sighting, simply move the instrument to the second station and again use the Sun. If the Sun is not available, then, using the theodolite at the first station, establish a stake on the line of the two stations, but about 1000 feet away, and sight on this from the second station. Either method makes a plumb bob unnecessary and avoids very careful centring over a tack in the top of the peg. Time is more expensive in the field than in the office. The necessary Sun observations, including a double check, can be made in less than 10 minutes. Always make three determinations. If on reducing them the first two differ one can fall back on the third.

The two essential levels on a theodolite are the cross bubble parallel to the trunnion axis and the alidade bubble at right angles to this. Theodolites differ in the manner in which the latter is controlled. In many older instruments the whole vertical unit lifts out of the trunnions. On such an instrument the so-called clip screws for adjustment necessarily move the whole unit, telescope, circle, verniers, and bubble. Here the bubble has to be centralized before intersecting the object being sighted. But in modern instruments the bubble and telescope are controlled separately, so that an adjustment of the bubble can be made *after* the object has been intersected, but before the vertical circle is read.

Instrument makers cannot centre the circles of a theodolite with an accuracy comparable to that with which the graduating engine cuts the divisions, but if both verniers are read the average will be free of centring errors. Theodolites with optical reading devices automatically eliminate this error, which in any case is unlikely to affect our work. However, in measuring profiles more accuracy is needed in vertical than in horizontal angles, and so it is advisable that at each site at least one terrestrial object should have its altitude determined accurately, by reading both vertical circle verniers on both faces. Provided the bubble has been accurately set on both pointings, the over-all mean will be correct and so can be used to obtain the index error on, say, vernier C face right. The other points on the profile need then be measured only on face right, vernier C. Naturally this index error will be determined before leaving home, and if any serious change takes place the cause must be sought and matters put right. No force should ever be applied to any part of the vertical system other than the bare minimum needed for operation.

Never measure altitudes when the surrounding ground has been heated by a strong sun and never when the ray passes close under or over an intermediate cloud. On one occasion when the ray passed through the underside of a layer of mist the author watched the altitude of a distant point change by 10 arc minutes in a few minutes of time. The change was steadily progressive, as was shown by half a dozen readings.

If the line of collimation of the telescope is not accurately at right angles to the trunnion axis, but is in error by c, horizontal angles will be affected by $c/\cos h$, where h is the altitude. It follows that if h is always small the effect will be constant and so will produce no error provided the face is not changed. On the other hand, if *all* horizontal angles are taken on both faces the elimination of this error is complete. This elaboration is seldom necessary, but when h is large, as with a high Sun, it is safer to use both faces unless c is known to be small.

A side tilt i of the vertical axis is another matter, as this produces an error $i \tan h$, which will not be eliminated by a change of face. For this reason when observing the Sun the instrument must be accurately levelled. If for any cause, such as soft ground, the cross bubble shows a sign of movement, do not touch the foot screws but read the dislevelment at each sight and apply the correction. If the right-hand end is high deduct $i \tan h$ from the horizontal circle reading.

B.2. Procedure at a site

Set up and level the theodolite and clamp the lower motion. Thereafter do not touch the foot screws or the lower tangent screw. Now read the plate bearing (P.B.) of a distant well-defined object, hereinafter called the Referring Object (R.O.). Bring the Sun into the field and note the time to the nearest second when the limb (either limb) touches the vertical wire. Read the plate and the cross bubble. Repeat on the other limb. Repeat the whole operation on the other face and check on the R.O.

If there is hurry, e.g. if the Sun is threatened by cloud, a good rapid determination of azimuth can be made by bisecting the Sun's disc instead of reading on each limb. Many years of experience have shown that this method is capable of giving an accuracy of $\pm 1'$, but the beginner had better take both limbs, afterwards using the average time with the average plate reading. If, owing to cloud, a reading is obtained on one limb only, it can be used if the plate reading is corrected by $s/\cos h$, where s is the Sun's semidiameter. h must be read or estimated.

B.3. Calculating the azimuth

An example is given in Table B.1. The Sun was low and there were clouds about. Accordingly it was decided to use one face only. The working is given for two half-sets (the term set is best reserved for a complete set with a half-set taken on each face). In each both limbs were used. The observed times and plate bearings are given. The mean time is corrected for the watch error, thus obtaining G.M.T. The next line is the Greenwich Hour Angle taken from the Nautical Almanac for the previous *even* hour. This is followed by the correction for the number of minutes and seconds elapsed since the even hour. Applying the longitude gives the local hour angle H. To obtain the Sun's azimuth A we use

$$\cot A = \sin \phi / \tan H - \cos \phi \tan \delta / \sin H = N - M.$$

Deducting the corresponding mean plate bearing (P.B.) gives the azimuth of the plate zero (A.P.Z.). The azimuth of any object observed from this set-up is then obtained by adding its P.B. to A.P.Z., always watching that P.B.R.O. has not changed.

We see in Table B.1 that the two results differ by only 0'·4. A later and more careful determination showed that the mean was probably within 1 arc minute of the truth. It will also be seen that the total time taken was not much more than 5 minutes.

Table B.1. *Example of determination of azimuth of a notch*

Temple Wood
Set up in small group Q
R.O. is notch behind circle

Lat. ϕ	56° 7'·4			
Long.	5 29 ·9 w			
Date	15 October 1968			

R.O.		248° 7' 40"			248° 7' 20"	
IO	15h 57min 24s	154 38 40	16h 0min 59s	156 3 30		
OI	15 58 19	155 26 0	16 2 27	155 50 0		
Φ	15 57 51	155 2 20	16 1 43	155 56 45		
Fast	59 57		59 57			
G.M.T.	14 57 54		15 1 46			

Even hour	33° 34'·0	33° 34'·0	
minutes	14 15 ·0	15 15 ·0	
seconds	13 ·5	11 ·5	
G.H.A.	48 2 ·5	49 0 ·5	
Long.	5 29 ·9	5 29 ·9	
H	42 32 ·6	43 30 ·6	
decl.	−8 41 ·4	−8 41 ·4	

$\cos \phi$	0·55741	0·55741
$\tan \delta$	−0·15284	−0·15284
$\sin H\,(\div)$	0·67615	0·68848
M	−0·12600	−0·12374

$\sin \phi$	0·83024	0·83024
$\tan H\,(\div)$	0·91772	0·94930
N	0·90468	0·87458
M	−0·12600	−0·12374

$\cot A = (N-M)$	1·03068	0·99832
A	224° 8'·1	225° 2'·9
P.B.	155 2 ·3	155 56 ·7
A.P.Z.	69 5 ·8	69 6 ·2

Mean A.P.Z.	69° 6'·0
P.B.R.O.	248 7 ·5
Az. R.O.	317 13 ·5

A later determination using both faces gave 317° 12'·6.

P.B. = bearing read on plate (horizontal circle)
A.P.Z. = azimuth of plate zero
R.O. = referring object
H = local hour angle of Sun

B.4. No Sun

The above-described method of determining azimuth is the most satisfactory. But, if the Sun does not appear, a distant point like a mountain top can sometimes be used, provided it can be identified on the Ordnance Survey with certainty. The most satisfactory is a cairn or triangulation station, since the coordination can be found unambiguously from the large-scale maps. If geographical coordinates (latitude and longitude) have to be used, the method of calculating the azimuth will be found in Thom 1967, p. 24. But if grid coordinates can be obtained the calculation is much simpler, and will be found in the appendix to the same work. For lunar lines the azimuths will be needed to one or two minutes, and for this accuracy the point used will need to be more than 5 miles distant, even if the 6-in O.S. maps are available.

B.5. The ground plan

Every stone within easy reach of the theodolite can now be put in by measuring the distance and plate bearing of each corner. Make a sketch of the plan of the stone (near the ground) facing the theodolite. If the stone is small it is normally sufficient to take the plate bearing of the two apparent edges and the distances to the nearest and furthest points on the stone at ground level. Into the 'box' so produced on the drawing table the sketch will enable the plan to be drawn. But for large important stones and upright slabs take all corners and determine the azimuth of the faces. This is easily done by sighting along a face to a distant object—there is sure to be some mark that can be held by the eye till it can be sighted over the 'open' telescope sights. Repeat, looking the other way, and make sure that the two bearings so found differ by something very close to 180°.

If it is necessary to contour an extensive site make use of the theodolite as a tacheometer. It is sure to have stadia wires on the diaphragm. All that is needed at a small site is to mark a bamboo rod with a rag at the height of the telescope. The rod is then held at a few spots scattered over the site and the plate bearing and altitude of the rag read on the circles. With the distance also measured the rest is office work.

It is often necessary to run a traverse. If the ground is uneven great care must be taken with the chaining. It often saves time to measure a base line and triangulate, especially if much chaining has to be done on the slope.

APPENDIX C

Profiles from the Ordnance Survey maps

WHEN it is desired to construct the profile of distant hills or mountains from a contoured map, the following method may be used.

Choose a point P on or near a hilltop. If the map has the National Grid superimposed, P is conveniently chosen as a grid intersection point. Calculate the distance D_0 of P from the site S. Also calculate the azimuth of P from S and of S from P. Draw through P a fine pencil line at this last azimuth. On each contour find a point B at which a line from S is tangent. In practice one takes the point on the contour furthest from PS. Let $D = D_0 - PN$. Then from S the azimuth of B is greater than

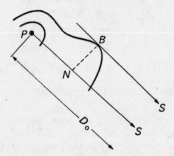

FIG. C.1. Constructing a profile.

the azimuth of P by $3438 \times BN/D$ arc minutes. The apparent altitude of B from S is found by (3.7) or (3.8). If the area being covered is large, BN may be too great for the above approximation, and new positions will be taken for P. The fact that SB is in general inclined, and so cannot really be tangent to the contour, which is by definition horizontal, introduces no appreciable error because in practice we are dealing with small inclinations.

The greatest care must be taken to make sure that no intervening ridge hides the profile. Only a visit to the site can ensure that in the immediate vicinity of the site the view is clear.

In considering the accuracy of the profile so obtained remember that even accurately surveyed contours can tell nothing about what happens between two consecutive lines. It follows that, using, for example, the 1-in O.S. with contours at 50-foot intervals, theoretically the greatest error might be nearly 50 feet, which is 3 arc minutes at 10 miles. Before assuming that there can never be an error as large as this, find out by inspection or otherwise if the contours have been surveyed or interpolated. Greater distances certainly give greater accuracy to the *shape* of a profile, but long lines are likely to have low or even negative altitudes and so may be badly affected be refraction. This is well brought out in Fig. 9.2.

If it turns out that a constructed profile contains lunar foresights it ought to be measured by theodolite at the first opportunity.

LIST OF DISTRICTS

THIS list shows the prefixes used in the reference numbers given to the various sites. These numbers are the same as those used in *Megalithic sites in Britain*, which contains a full list of prefixes on p. 167.

H 1	Lewis	A 4	Kintyre	P 4	Fife
H 3	N. Uist	A 6	Jura	G 3	Wigtownshire E
		A 10	Kerry and L.	G 9	Midlothian
M 1	Mull N		Fyne E	„	East Lothian
M 2	„ S			„	Berwick
M 4	Tiree	N 1	Caithness	„	Peebles
A 2	Argyll	P 1	Perth W of Tay	L 1	Cumberland
A 3	Knapdale	P 3	Forfar	W 9	Pembroke

BIBLIOGRAPHY

DRYDEN, SIR H., BT., Original MS. Surveys, property of the Society of Antiquaries of Scotland (1871).

GODFREY, H., *An elementary treatise on the lunar theory*. Macmillan (1859).

JAMES, COL. SIR HENRY, *Plans and photographs of Stonehenge and of Turusachan in the Island of Lewis with notes relating to the Druids, etc.* Ordnance Survey (1867).

KEILLER, A., *Windmill Hill and Avebury*. Clarendon Press, Oxford (1965).

MITCHELL, H., *Pitlochry district, its topography, archaeology and history*. L. Mackay, Pitlochry (1923).

SITTER, W. DE, On the system of astronomical constants. *Bull. astr. Insts Neth.* **8**, 213 (1938).

SOMERVILLE, B., Astronomical indications in the Megalithic monument at Callanish. *J. Br. astr. Ass.* **23**, 83 (1912).

—— Prehistoric monuments in the Outer Hebrides and their astronomical significance. *J.R. anthrop. Inst. Gt Br. Irel.* **42**, N.S. **15** (1912).

THOM, A., The solar observatories of Megalithic man. *J. Br. astr. Ass.* **64**, 397 (1954).

—— An empirical investigation of atmospheric refraction. *Emp. surv. Rev.* **14**, 248 (1958).

—— The larger units of length of Megalithic man. *Jl R. statist. Soc.* A **127**, 527 (1964).

—— Megalithic astronomy: indications in standing stones. *Vistas Astr.* **7**, 1 (1965).

—— Megaliths and mathematics. *Antiquity* **40**, 121 (1966).

—— *Megalithic sites in Britain*. Clarendon Press, Oxford (1967).

—— The metrology and geometry of cup and ring marks. *Systematics* **6**, 173 (1968).

—— The lunar observatories of Megalithic man. *Vistas Astr.* **11**, 1 (1969).

—— The geometry of cup and ring marks. *Trans. ancient Monument Soc.* **16**, 77 (1969).

AUTHOR INDEX

SUBJECT INDEX